THE OFFICIAL
COMPANION
SEASON THREE

D1379352

BATTLESTAR GALACTICA:
THE OFFICIAL COMPANION SEASON THREE

ISBN: 1 84576 478 1
ISBN-13: 9781845764784

Published by
Titan Books
A division of
Titan Publishing Group Ltd
144 Southwark St
London, SE1 0UP

First edition August 2007
2 4 6 8 10 9 7 5 3 1

ACKNOWLEDGEMENTS

The author would like to thank the cast and crew of *Battlestar Galactica* for providing another Companion-load of insightful thoughts, information and amusing anecdotes, in-between delivering an unforgettable season of groundbreaking TV drama.

Special praise goes to the series' guiding lights, Ron Moore and David Eick, and the show's writing staff, especially David Weddle, Bradley Thompson and Mark Verheiden, for their patient handling of each and every question (and follow-up question... and follow-up follow-up question) sent their way. Other crewmembers worthy of a Colonial salute for their above-and-beyond-the-call-of-duty contributions to this book include Michael Rymer, Doug McLean, Gary Hutzel, Bear McCreary and Glenne Campbell, while Jamie Bamber gets a Medal of Distinction for writing his brilliant foreword.

My thanks also go to *Battlestar Galactica*'s unit publicist Carol Marks-George, whose scheduling and logistical skills would put a Cylon Hybrid to shame, and to the unit photographer responsible for the images that illustrate the *Battlestar Galactica* Companions, Carole Segal. Further kudos goes to Maril Davis and James Halpern at Universal, Lana Kim at Sci Fi and Daniel McPeek at Universal Licensing for their vital roles in making this book possible.

At Titan Books, I must pay tribute to the outstanding work of my champion editor, Cath Trechman, and designer Russell Seal, plus their esteemed colleagues Jo Boylett and Adam Newell. And on a personal note, I'd like to thank Ian Calcutt, Toby Weidmann, Jayne, Joan, Joanna, Danny, Dad and Mum for their various contributions.

DEDICATION
For my grandparents, Terry and Doris McMahon — never forgotten.

Visit our website:
www.titanbooks.com

Did you enjoy this book? We love to hear from our readers. Please e-mail us at:
readerfeedback@titanemail.com or write to Reader Feedback at the above address.

To subscribe to our regular newsletter for up-to-the-minute news, great offers and competitions, email: **titan-news@titanemail.com**

A CIP catalogue record for this title is available from the British Library.

Printed and bound in the USA.

BATTLESTAR GALACTICA

THE OFFICIAL
COMPANION
SEASON THREE

DAVID BASSOM

TITAN BOOKS

[CONTENTS]

This is my first foreword. I have some experience with four *letter* words… but I don't suppose that will help here. Frak. Or perhaps it will… I must just say how thrilled I was when David Bassom called me and asked me to introduce this latest *Official Companion* to my adored *Battlestar Galactica*. Titan Books have shared every step of this incredible journey with us. These pages document not only what it is to watch this show and follow these rich characters on their quest for a new identity, but they also capture what it is to make this show, to live it. When I am old and foggy I will always be able to stagger to my bookshelf and in one arm-stretch I will be back in Vancouver 2006. I will be back in season three, our best and most ambitious to date, which saw the fleet try to settle in a new home, which brought us inside the Cylon mind for the first time, and which ends in courtroom denial and revelations of enemies within. For that, David, I thank you.

The beginning of each new season is about questions. Mainly these questions concern how Ron Moore, David Eick and our tireless writers have made sense of the

mess they invariably left behind when they decided to let the cliff hang, or, in this case, the year jump at the end of the previous season. But among the *Galactica* family of cast and crew there are other recurring intrigues; for example, which continent will James Callis fly in from? Will Eddie Olmos' moustache need counselling before its further demise? How much more miserable can success make David Eick? How many kids will Bamber have now? In essence it is back to school…

Telling a story on series television forces you to experience changes in your own personal life parallel to the fictional changes your character undergoes in his dramatic life. And when that fictive story is *Battlestar Galactica* each of those lives unfolds in near to real time. In effect these last four years I have been on two odysseys; one of them describes the tumultuous saga that Lee Adama has been thrown into and the other the more mundane progress of Jamie Bamber. Doing a play on the stage one lives an entire life in a single evening, on the big screen it might take a few months, but with a true television epic like *Battlestar Galactica* the character ages and grows apace with the actor. And that is what

has happened to me and to Lee, to Mary and Laura, to James and Gaius, to Eddie and Bill.

When I watch the miniseries, which as of writing we shot four years ago, I see a sequence where a young viper pilot lands for the first time aboard the Battlestar *Galactica*; he is apprehensive, ill at ease and walks with a forced confidence. I watch the character and I describe the actor. I remember landing in Vancouver in the spring of 2003 desperate to hide the sense of intimidation I felt at playing my first lead role on American television. I so wanted my accent to fit, my walk to swagger and to own the call-sign I had somehow inherited. If Lee is shrill and reactionary when he first encounters Adama it might have something to do with the feeling of dislocation Jamie felt when first confronted with the deep conviction of Olmos in the makeup trailer. So when at the end of this third season Lee is able to lock his father's gaze in his witness-stand paroxysm it might be because the actor, like the character, has found his voice. In the time it has taken Lee to understand his father

I, Jamie, have become a father three times over and, I dare say, have come to understand my own father one heck of a lot better.

But it is not just the actors and characters that have been in a strange dance through time. The Colonial fleet we depict has been waltzing and stumbling with the western society we inhabit. Together we have elected new leaders, gone to war, contemplated our own destruction and often contributed to it.

In this third season in particular I have been so proud of the boldness with which our stories have taken the hardest of news stories and found the truth that only fiction provides. We watched beloved characters and friends decide to turn themselves into human bombs just when our most feared enemies were doing the same on London's buses. On our news networks we watched as a dictator was put on the stand and executed by his former subjects, whilst on *Galactica* a collaborator-President was similarly tried but surprised to be acquitted by his. It is only by empathizing with those we would otherwise find abhorrent that we can ever hope to understand the situation or hope to find the path out.

And that's what good drama lets us do. It allows us to see and to feel things we otherwise would not. And great drama allows us to do that on every level: the psychological, the personal and the political. I am proud to say in the paired down world of *Battlestar Galactica* there is no plot, no character and no relationship that does not breathe the oxygen of all three levels at once.

If this journey has been both personal and epic, real and fictional, there are thanks to those who made it so: firstly to Ron Moore and David Eick for turning empty space into the richest human petri-dish on screen and for allowing actors and directors the space to create and to grow. To our amazing writing staff for keeping the corridors of *Galactica* winding and surprising. To the deepest cast on television. To our Canadian crew who make it happen. To our LA based post-production team who make it shine. To Anthony and Resho for making it delicious. To Bear for giving us goose-bumps. And to Harvey Frand, the genial ringmaster of this astral circus.

Special thanks go to my friends Michael Rymer, Mary McDonnell and Edward James Olmos who set the collaborative tone and to whose enthusiasm, integrity and talent our young cast has always aspired. They more than anyone have taught me who I can be in this life and in this craft and I love them for it. A heartfelt mention too to James Callis, my fellow Londoner, for pinching me when it seems too good.

But perhaps most of all I thank Paramedic Ishay and my three characters at home, Buckets, Bava and Paalump, for living every step with me.

Thank you *Battlestar Galactica*: a lesson in life.

Jamie Bamber
April 2007

[BEYOND NEW CAPRICA]

162A EXT. NEW CAPRICA - STREET - DAY

CYLON CENTURIONS are MARCHING through the streets. The PEOPLE of New Caprica are standing on the sidelines, watching them in shock, some with tears rolling down their cheeks - it's like watching the Nazis march into Paris.

FIND Tigh and Ellen in the crowd... then Laura, who looks shaken to her core — everything she's feared has just come to pass and she's perhaps the most heart-broken of them all...

162B EXT./INT. KARA'S TENT — DAY

LEOBEN pulls aside the tent flap and finds Anders still in bed, looking feverish.

                    LEOBEN
          I'm looking for Kara Thrace.

Anders doesn't answer, looks up at Leoben with surprise and fear. Leoben waits a beat, then steps into the tent and begins to move toward Anders...

162C EXT. NEW CAPRICA - STREET - DAY

Where we find Kara and Tyrol standing together.

                    TYROL
          What do we do here, Captain?

                    KARA
          Same thing we always do.
              (beat)
          We fight 'em until we can't.

As Kara and Tyrol watch the Cylons marching in...

SUPER: TO BE CONTINUED...

                                        FADE OUT.

                    <u>END EPISODE</u>

{BEYOND NEW CAPRICA}

> "The end of season two gave us an opportunity to re-invigorate the series and its character dynamics, and really go into exciting new territory in season three..." — Ronald D. Moore

O ne. Year. Later. With three simple words during the closing moments of its second season, series head writer/executive producer Ronald D. Moore had radically redesigned the landscape of *Battlestar Galactica* and once again challenged viewers' perceptions of the series. By moving the storyline forward a year, to the Cylons' invasion of New Caprica, Moore had also succeeded in giving season two a stunning cliffhanger ending that would provide a rich and intriguing starting point for the third season.

While the series' writing staff had briefly discussed story ideas and possibilities for *Battlestar Galactica*'s third season during the final weeks of production on season two, work on the new twenty-episode season really began with a lengthy informal meeting between Moore and *Battlestar Galactica*'s other showrunner, executive producer David Eick. The unusual setting for this meeting? Disney World, Florida.

"Just like we did at the start of season two, Ron and I wanted to have a meeting in a casual environment where we could discuss in broad terms what the season was going to be," Eick explains. "My friend Breck Eisner had kindly got us passes to the private area at Disney World where we could go for a drink; so we just figured, what better way to start season three than to go drink scotch, ride Space Mountain and then watch Monday Night Football at the ESPN Club?

"Ron and I came up with a number of ideas at Disney World. We talked about doing a few episodes dealing with the occupation of New Caprica and the idea of jumping forward in time at the start of the season, to the point where things had gone awry between the humans and the Cylons. We also discussed the escape from New Caprica and how everyone would then try to resume their old lives on the *Galactica*, and we talked about broad arcs for the characters.

"Another thing we discussed was the need to take a fresh and unusual approach to the overall storytelling in season three," Eick reveals. "Ron looked at me and told me there was a certain boredom to some of the storylines we were trying to do in season

Below: Whereas season two resolved the previous year's cliffhanger with a lengthy seven-episode arc, *Battlestar Galactica's* makers chose to wrap the New Caprica story arc with the opening three episodes of season three.

Above: While the New Caprica story arc would be resolved relatively quickly, the effects of the Colonials' settlement on the planet would be felt throughout season three.

two — and he wanted to address that. From there, we began to discuss not just story-lines involving the Cylons but telling stories from the Cylons' point of view — possibly going into a Cylon Baseship with our characters as prisoners and getting into the Cylon world on a deeper level."

Following their casual story conference at Disney World, Moore and Eick continued to develop their plans for season three with *Battlestar Galactica*'s writing staff. Collectively, the group would devise the storylines for the season's opening instalments (from 'Occupation' to 'A Measure of Salvation'), in preparation for the episodes' scripting. On learning that the US Sci Fi Channel was keen for the New Caprica arc to be wrapped as quickly as possible, Moore settled on the idea of resolving the plot-line in a trilogy of episodes. The considerable expense of shooting exterior location scenes for the New Caprica sequences also made a short story arc appealing.

"In hindsight, I feel the New Caprica storyline was about the right length," Moore notes. "I appreciate New Caprica was a rich environment that you could have told many other stories in, but I don't know that the series should have become planet-bound for an extended period of time, because then it's not *Battlestar Galactica*. The sit-uation also meant that the *Galactica* had to be sidelined throughout that arc until the end. So I always felt we'd have a short leash on how long we could spend on New Caprica and geared my thinking towards a fairly short arc. I always wanted us to get back into space and resume the search for Earth."

As the New Caprica storyline took shape, it quickly began to provide the basis of

Above: Saul Tigh's story arc in season three grew out of Ronald D. Moore's desire to utilize the character more effectively than had been done in the latter part of season two.

a major storyline for the *Galactica*'s Executive Officer. "I was really excited about what we came up with for Tigh, because I didn't feel we had used him effectively during the latter part of season two," Moore notes. "So I was really pleased about all the changes and shocks we came up with for the character."

Going into season three, Moore and Eick always knew they wanted to fill the key blanks created by the year-jump forward at the end of season two — such as the disintegration of Lee Adama and Kara Thrace's relationship. While the writing staff initially discussed the possibility of threading a series of New Caprica flashbacks through the early episodes of season three, they quickly decided it would be more effective and less confusing to group the flashbacks into one episode — which later became 'Unfinished Business'.

"As we were only going to be using the New Caprica sets for the opening episodes, we knew we would have to shoot the flashbacks at the same time," Moore explains. "So I said, 'Okay, let's dedicate a day of production to shooting the flashbacks that we'll put into later episodes.' But as we kept talking about how we were going to use those flashbacks, we quickly moved away from the idea of scattering the flashbacks between episodes and settled on doing a specific storyline for flashbacks."

With the resolution of the New Caprica storyline in place, the writers focused on the other story arc that would dominate the first half of season three: the Cylon Basestar plotline. Although the writing staff had briefly discussed the possibility of a Cylon Basestar storyline in season two, the concept only really started to take shape when it was noted that Baltar could temporarily find himself imprisoned on a Basestar, following events on New Caprica. Baltar's time on the Basestar presented an opportunity for the character to start wondering if he himself was a Cylon — a story idea Moore had originally suggested in his pre-season one Series Bible. The Cylon Basestar story arc also allowed the writers to establish that the Cylons had become interested in finding Earth for themselves.

"The race to Earth was an idea we talked about doing at the end of season two," Moore confirms. "It came back to us when we were mapping out the first episodes of season three."

At Eick's suggestion, the Cylon arc was designed to involve the return of two-time guest star (and former *Xena: Warrior Princess* star) Lucy Lawless as D'Anna Biers, a.k.a. the Cylon Number Three. "I felt we would do well to bring Lucy Lawless back into the fold at the beginning of season three because I thought she would give us a shot in the arm in terms of broadening our audience, with her fans," Eick explains. "The return of her character also nicely dovetailed into this multi-episode arc we were planning. So we talked to Lucy and quickly settled on the idea of her doing ten episodes of the season."

Above: Gaius Baltar's temporary imprisonment on a Cylon Basestar provided the basis of a multi-episode Cylon story arc — and also enabled the series to focus on the long-brewing question of whether Baltar is a Cylon.

"Putting Baltar on the Basestar and watching him twist D'Anna around his little finger really pulled that story together," adds co-executive producer Mark Verheiden. "The D'Anna finding God/being 'boxed' arc gradually developed as we started writing episodes, coming together in an especially perverse way with her repeated suicides."

To ensure that the series' depiction of Cylon life was in keeping with his original vision, Moore wrote a document for the show's cast and crew entitled *Life on the Cylon Baseship*. Moore's main revelations included the idea that the already known 'Significant Seven' Cylons were programmed not to think about the remaining, mysterious 'Final Five' Cylons.

By deciding to explore the Cylon world in season three, both Moore and Eick were aware that they would undermine the characters' mystery and were also propelling *Battlestar Galactica* into a much more traditional science fiction realm than it had previously existed in. But despite the reservations of several cast and crewmembers, they remained convinced it was the right direction for the show to go in.

"I remember Jamie Bamber was one of the people who was very concerned about the Basestar arc," Eick recalls. "He said to me, 'In *Jaws* you barely saw the shark — and that's what made the shark mysterious.' I thought he had a valid concern, but my response to Jamie was, 'If *Jaws* had been a forty-hour movie, you can bet we would have gone home with the shark and we would have met the shark's wife and kids!' There's a difference between a movie and a TV series, especially one that is entering its third season. You have to be willing to take risks in an ongoing series, to keep it fresh."

"Personally, I felt you could only milk the mystery of the Cylons so long and so far," adds Moore. "It seemed like we were getting to know the Cylons more and more as time went on anyway. I felt there was more to be gained by understanding and developing their society, rather than keeping them opaque and mysterious. If we'd kept the Cylons as mysterious figures who cause problems for our main characters every once in a while, that would have kept them from ever becoming three-dimensional. You couldn't play the pathos of being a Cylon or truly understand their motivation without getting to know them more."

Like with season two, *Battlestar Galactica*'s producers knew that the US Sci Fi Channel planned to air season three in two blocks of ten episodes, so 'The Eye of

Below: The decision to explore life on a Cylon Basestar divided the series' cast and crew — but was vigorously defended by Ron Moore and fellow executive producer David Eick.

Jupiter' and 'Rapture' were devised as a story arc-focused, mid-season two-parter. To address the Sci Fi Channel's concerns about the series' story arcs making it inaccessible to casual viewers or newcomers, *Battlestar Galactica*'s producers also agreed that the middle section of season three would include a number of stand-alone instalments. This led to the development of such episodes as 'Hero', 'The Woman King', 'A Day in the Life' and 'Dirty Hands'.

"We promised the network we would do stand-alones that wouldn't be so dependent on prior knowledge of the show," Moore confirms. "So we gave them that but tried to work in other serialized elements along the way and balance the storyline out."

The closing episodes of season three developed naturally in the writing room. The trial of Gaius Baltar was a logical outcome of earlier events in the series and was initially set to take place across episodes thirteen and fourteen, until Moore embraced co-executive producer Michael Angeli's suggestion that Baltar's trial should be the season-ending "trial of the century". Similarly, the death and mysterious return of Kara Thrace resulted from an idea Moore suggested during the development of 'Maelstrom'. Moore readily acknowledges the latter story arc is a familiar staple of the traditional space opera and might seem at odds with *Battlestar Galactica*'s mission to reinvent small-screen science fiction.

"We did have concerns about that," Moore states. "We talked about it at length,

THE LOST ARC

During the planning of the episodes leading to the third-season finale, the writing staff developed an elaborate back-story that was set to be revealed during Baltar's trial. This back-story involved a shocking incident that took place during President Baltar's rule on New Caprica.

"The idea was that a group of Sagittarons had moved away from the rest of the Colony and started a successful, private farm collective," reveals Mark Verheiden. "When a blight wiped out the crops for the rest of the Colony, a group of hardliners — who hated the Sagittarons anyway — stormed the Sagittarons' camp, murdered them all and took their food stores. The massacre was never prosecuted and the escape from New Caprica soon took precedence over everything else.

"One of the reasons for this story was to show another side of President Baltar's reign on New Caprica. In the original idea he — and the Cylons — had actually tried to stop the slaughter, so that was going to help exonerate Baltar when he eventually came to trial. In the Sagittaron massacre storyline, we would have discovered that the Cylons, who came to be blamed (with Baltar) for the deaths, had ironically tried to prevent them."

Ultimately, this Sagittaron story arc was abandoned during the scripting of season three's two-part finale, 'Crossroads'. "We just realized we didn't need the Sagittaron storyline, so we dropped it," says Ronald D. Moore. "I think the biggest mistake we made in season three was committing so much time and effort to this storyline which we never needed." ■

but in the end we decided Kara's death and return just fit the larger mythology of the show — what's really going on with the Cylons, the one true God, the Lords of Kobol, her destiny, etc. It fit the pieces pretty well, even though it was something that had been done in sci-fi before."

In an effort to make Kara's death seem as convincing as possible, the producers decided to remove Sackhoff's screen credit from the title sequence of the closing three episodes. "I think we all knew some people would still guess that Starbuck would return at some point," Moore admits. "But I feel we did play that card as well as we could and fooled a lot of the audience."

Kara's return would form part of season three's stunning ending, alongside the revelation of four Cylons. Moore hatched this idea during the development of the season's closing six episodes.

"It came up in the writers' room because I didn't feel we had enough surprises and twists for the finale," Moore explains. "We weren't moving the show forward enough or setting up enough things for season four. So I came up with the idea that

NETWORK NEWS

The US Sci Fi Channel had a clear idea of what it wanted from *Battlestar Galactica*'s third season. "First and foremost, we wanted a continuation and build on everything the show had already achieved," explains Sci Fi executive Mark Stern. "We wanted to see the characters grow, the challenges they're facing build and never get the feeling that we were treading water.

"It was also very important for us to get our family of characters back together and into space as quickly as possible," he reveals. "We wanted to re-establish the franchise as soon as was feasible, without rushing anything."

Stern reports that Sci Fi was particularly excited about Moore's plans for a Cylon story arc in season three, the "mindblowing" events surrounding the revelation of four Cylons among the *Galactica* crew, and Kara Thrace's death and return. He also acknowledges the main specific sources of discussion between Sci Fi and the producers in season three concerned the plotline of 'Collaborators', Adama and Roslin's 'getting high' scene in 'Unfinished Business' and Baltar's torture in 'Taking a Break From All Your Worries'.

"Probably the main thing I talk to Ron and David about is Sci Fi's desire to keep the show moving towards being hopeful and uplifting and not allowing the darker elements to consume the storytelling," Stern notes. "That may be where we've been the most helpful. I think we've settled in a pretty comfortable rhythm with them. There weren't so many knock-down arguments this season compared to previous seasons, where we had things like Sharon being attacked in 'Pegasus' and Adama killing the hybrid baby [in 'Valley of Darkness'].

"We've given Ron and David as much freedom as we can to take chances, and they've really pushed the envelope with the show," Stern states. "We're extremely happy with the show on a creative level. It has elevated the stature of the network." ■

four of our characters would start walking from different areas of the ship to the same room, look at each other and then say, 'We're Cylons'. From that shocking image, we started talking about who it would be and the implications of it."

The whole writing staff was involved in the selection of the four Cylons who would be revealed in the season finale. "That was really funny," Michael Angeli reveals. "We got together with Ron, put a bunch of names on the board and voted. Pretty much everyone's name was on the board, apart from Admiral Adama and President Laura — we didn't want them to be Cylons because we felt that would corrupt the show."

"In that discussion, we asked ourselves which of the characters would give us the most to play next season and whose back-story fitted in the most easily," Moore continues. "From that, I think our selections became quite obvious. Tyrol had found the Temple of Five on the algae planet, he had a religious background and he had unknowingly fallen in love with a Cylon, so he seemed to fit well. Anders had somehow survived two Resistance movements and had fallen for Kara, who the Cylons kept saying had a destiny, so it seemed an interesting place to take him. We knew little about Tory Foster, she was a bit of a blank slate, so that was an easy one.

"Tigh was the most problematic choice and I went back and forth on that all the way up to the shooting of the finale," Moore admits. "Tigh is among the most

Above: Kara Thrace's addition to the *Galactica*'s Memorial Wall was just one of the ways in which *Battlestar Galactica*'s producers tried to convince viewers of the character's permanent departure from the series.

Above: Samuel T. Anders' exposure as a Cylon grew from a casual idea Moore suggested for season three's finale.

human of our characters and he had gone through such personal angst, so I was concerned we were robbing something from the show by making him a Cylon. But I also thought it would be really interesting to see how he would react with the discovery he was a Cylon."

After working out believable back-stories for each of the newly discovered Cylons, the producers informed the real-life counterparts of Tigh, Tyrol, Anders and Tory about their characters' futures. "They were all a bit shocked," Moore says. "Aaron Douglas was probably the most hesitant, followed by Michael Hogan. But I think they all became cool with the idea in the end."

For its third season, *Battlestar Galactica*'s writing staff comprised of returning scribes Mark Verheiden, Bradley Thompson, David Weddle and Anne Cofell Saunders. The staff was completed by Michael Angeli, a writer/producer whose credits included *Medium*, *Dark Angel*, the 2003 revival of *The Twilight Zone* and the first season *Battlestar Galactica* episode 'Six Degrees of Separation', and former *Star Trek: Deep Space Nine* and *The Dead Zone* writer/producer Michael Taylor.

"The two Michaels were really good additions to the writing staff," says Moore. "They brought a certain richness of character and complicated ideas, in terms of who the characters were and where they were going. They also both got the voice of the show. Michael Angeli had done an episode for us before and was a known quality. I had read Michael Taylor's spec scripts and some of his other material, and knew him from *Star Trek*, and I thought he would be a good match."

All of *Battlestar Galactica*'s principal cast and crewmembers returned for the series' third season, along with the show's principal directors. To ensure the continued involvement of the show's most prolific director, Michael Rymer was signed up as a producer. "I wasn't available to do the season première, because I was doing another pilot [*A House Divided*] for a network," Rymer explains. "So David Eick came to me and said in exchange for me directing seven episodes I'd get a producer credit and fee. David and Ron wanted to have me around the set, because they didn't think they would be around so much."

Season three of *Battlestar Galactica* began shooting on April 10 2006, with

production once again based at Vancouver Film Studios. As with the previous season, season three was shot in two blocks of ten episodes, which were separated by a one-month hiatus.

Above: All of *Battlestar Galactica's* principal cast and crewmembers returned for season three.

In a change from the series' previous year, Sci Fi earmarked season three for an October première. This would pitch *Battlestar Galactica* against first-run network television offerings and would also enable season three to be broadcast over the course of six months, with a brief (rather than three-month-long) mid-season break.

Season three's US début was preceded by a one-hour clip-show, *Battlestar Galactica: The Story So Far*. Narrated by Mary McDonnell, the recap documentary aired across various NBC Universal television channels, including Sci Fi, USA, Sleuth, Bravo and Universal HD, and was also made available via iTunes and various websites. Further interest in the return of *Battlestar Galactica* would be generated by Sci Fi's launch of 'The Resistance', the series' first original online spin-off drama... ■

[THE RESISTANCE]

WRITERS: Bradley Thompson & David Weddle
DIRECTOR: Wayne Rose

CAST: Michael Hogan (Saul Tigh), Aaron Douglas (Galen Tyrol), Nicki Clyne (Cally Henderson-Tyrol), Matthew Bennett (Aaron Doral), Christian Tessier (Tucker 'Duck' Clellan), Dominic Zamprogna (James 'Jammer' Lyman), Emily Holmes (Nora), Alisen Down (Jean Barolay), Carmen Moore (Sister Tivenan)

"We need more people or this Resistance movement is going to die in its crib!" — Saul Tigh

During the second month of the Cylon occupation of New Caprica, Saul Tigh and Galen Tyrol are keen to recruit new members of the fledgling Resistance movement. At Tigh's suggestion, Tyrol and a former member of his Deck Gang, James 'Jammer' Lyman, try to enlist the support of former Viper pilot Tucker 'Duck' Clellan. But Duck declines the offer, as he is hoping to start a family with his wife, Nora.

Nora and Cally Henderson-Tyrol are praying in the temple when Cylons arrive in search of weapons that have been hidden in the building by the Resistance. In the confrontation that follows, the Cylon Centurions open fire and kill ten people — including Nora.

Following the Cylon assault on the temple, Jammer is questioned at the Cylon Detention Center. Aaron Doral outlines his vision of peaceful co-existence between humans and Cylons on New Caprica and invites Jammer to join the New Caprica Police. While Jammer is reluctant to sign up, Doral leaves a contact chip with him in case he changes his mind.

Devastated by Nora's death, Duck tells Tyrol he has joined the New Caprica Police — to find out who informed the Cylons about the weapons in the Temple. As Duck contemplates his dangerous plans, Jammer finds himself considering Doral's offer...

The US Sci Fi Channel initially began exploring the possibility of producing original, online *Battlestar Galactica* dramatic content during the series' second season. Following a number of casual discussions with the series' producers about the viability of making exclusive, website-delivered 'mini' episodes (dubbed 'webisodes'), the idea was raised again as plans for *Battlestar Galactica*'s third season took shape.

"When we talked about doing something to tie in with the launch of season three, we all very quickly settled on the idea of doing webisodes set between the end of season two and the start of season three, during the Cylon occupation of New Caprica," recalls Ronald D. Moore, who served as an executive producer on the project along with David

Eick. "That seemed like a natural choice to all of us. We agreed on the idea of doing ten webisodes of two to three minutes each, because two- to three-minute pieces are said to be ideal for people to download."

With the online spin-off's setting and format in place, Moore asked series producers David Weddle and Bradley Thompson to script its ten instalments. "Ron called Brad and I and said, 'You guys are going to write them because you've been here since the beginning and know the complete back-story of the characters and the world'," Weddle explains. "Sci Fi said it wanted the webisodes to take place during the Cylon occupation of New Caprica and to bridge the gap between the end of season two and the beginning of season three, to drum up interest in season three. We also knew we could only use Canadian actors because of the budgetary restrictions. Those were pretty much the parameters we had to work within.

"We had two days to come up with a plot for the webisodes," Weddle reveals. "The writing staff had already batted around a number of ideas of what they could be; we'd talked about ideas like a day in the life of Doc Cottle working out of his hospital tent, a day in the life of Gaeta working under Baltar's administration, the domestic life of Cally and Tyrol, and so on. But as Brad and I reviewed the scripts for the first four episodes of season three, we decided it would be more compelling to tell a single story that focused on the pivotal roles that two minor characters, Duck and Jammer, come to play in the opening episodes of season three."

"Duck and Jammer perform major actions in the opening episodes of season three, but we didn't see what drove them to those actions," continues Bradley Thompson. "When Ron wrote the episodes, he hinted at what made the characters do what they do, so we thought, 'That's the story!' It was a chance to broaden the storytelling and look at characters we don't have time to focus on in the broadcast series."

After deciding that the webisodes would provide the background to Duck and Jammer's respective transformations into a suicide bomber and a Cylon collaborator, Weddle and Thompson proceeded to develop the structure of the overall storyline. "To give the story unity, we decided Duck and Jammer should be friends — two guys who became close on New Caprica, but who were driven on divergent paths by a single tragic event: the Cylon raid on the temple," Weddle notes. "The Resistance's decision to hide weapons in the temple gave the drama the multifaceted moral complexity that we look for in all of our stories."

While developing the story arc for 'The Resistance' proved relatively straightforward, actually scripting the ten webisodes presented several unusual challenges. At Sci Fi's request, each instalment had to feature a storyline with a beginning, middle and end, as well as a hook/cliffhanger for the next webisode. During

SURVEILLANCE: ADDITIONAL

During the development of season three's opening episodes the roles of Duck and Jammer were actually reversed, with Duck becoming a collaborator and Jammer committing the suicide bombing. Their roles were later swapped by Ronald D. Moore, at the suggestion of Aaron Douglas. "Aaron pointed out that Jammer had been played as a weak guy in episodes like 'Valley of Darkness'," explains Moore. "So it just seemed a better way to go for those two characters."

SURVEILLANCE: ADDITIONAL

Following the making of 'The Resistance', the photo of Duck and Nora featured in 'Occupation' had to be digitally altered to show Emily Holmes' Nora alongside Christian Tessier as Duck. As the season three première was shot before the webisodes had been cast, the original picture featured another actress in the role.

their four days of scripting the web series (which was initially titled 'Crossroads', until Sci Fi retitled it 'The Resistance'), the writers were also restricted to using sets and locations that were featured in the opening episodes of season three.

"The tight budget meant that the webisodes were restricted to small character-based scenes," Weddle explains. "They were driven by dialogue and interpersonal conflict rather than spectacle or run-and-jump action sequences.

"You could say these were limitations, but we actually felt profoundly liberated by this," he insists. "We felt we could concentrate completely on the character dynamics and the moral issues the story raised. In the one action sequence we did write — the Cylon raid on the temple — we had the opportunity to emulate the work of some of our idols: Val Lewton, Jacques Tourneur, Edgar G. Ulmer and Fritz Lang. These film-makers knew that what you don't see on screen can often be even more compelling than what you do see."

Within days of the completion of Weddle and Thompson's twenty-two-page script, 'The Resistance' began a three-day shoot in *Battlestar Galactica*'s home turf of Vancouver. The webisodes were helmed by one of the series' regular second unit and first assistant directors, Wayne Rose, who had a lean six-strong crew at his disposal.

"I jumped at the chance to direct the webisodes," Rose says. "It was a good opportunity for me and it was exciting to do something the series had never done before. But I've got to admit, when we went into the project, I honestly don't think any of us had any idea what the end result would be like. Looking back, it was a hugely ambitious project given the resources we had and I think it's amazing we pulled this thing off.

"We were lucky in that we had access to the *Battlestar* series sets and the actors, and we used a lot of resources from the main unit — like the hair and makeup departments — when we were on location for the first day of the shoot. We actually shot alongside the main unit when we were on location; we were just thirty feet away and you could actually hear the director on our dailies!

"But in those three days, it seemed that everything that could go wrong did go wrong," Rose continues with a laugh. "For example, we were working with a Canon XL 100 HD camera that none of us had ever used before. It worked great on our first day, when we shot the exteriors, but then when we went on to the stage we found out the low light levels we use on the show meant the camera wouldn't focus. So we had the instruction manual out on the detention chamber set and the actors were sitting there while we tried to figure out how to make it work! It was pretty crazy."

The cast of 'The Resistance' was headed by *Battlestar Galactica* stars Michael Hogan, Aaron Douglas, Nicki Clyne and Matthew Bennett. "I was thrilled that the likes of Michael and Aaron were a part of the webisodes, because their involvement really added to it," Rose says. "Michael Hogan in particular was someone who really bought into the idea. He was very supportive from the beginning."

Hogan reports that he and his co-stars agreed to appear in 'The Resistance' out of loyalty to *Battlestar Galactica* and its makers. "When the producers first told me about the webisodes I told them if everyone was aboard and it was okay with the unions and agents and everyone, they could count me in," Hogan explains. "I'm committed to doing *Battlestar* and I'll support the show in any way I can.

"It was a fun experience," he continues. "It was like getting together with friends with a camera and making it up, because we all know the characters so well and it was easy to knock them out. I thought they turned out surprisingly well. The youngsters did amazing work."

"It was exciting to be a part of the webisodes," Aaron Douglas notes. "We were one of the first TV shows to do them and they turned out pretty cool. It was hard work doing them in-between the normal show, but it was great to expand the story and give some of the other actors, like Dominic and Christian, some more screen time."

'The Resistance' premièred during the five weeks running up to the début of *Battlestar Galactica*'s third season, with new webisodes

Above: Tigh loses an eye whilst being tortured by the Cylons because of his involvement with the Resistance.

being made available to US visitors to the Sci Fi website every Tuesday and Thursday. While Sci Fi had hoped to attract an audience of around 250,000, the first two episodes alone generated 1.8 million hits and the series is estimated to have scored more than seven million hits in total. The response to the webisodes was equally favourable, as 'The Resistance' was widely hailed a worthwhile addition to the *Battlestar Galactica* franchise.

"I'm proud of what the team did with the webisodes," says Moore. "Everyone worked above and beyond the call of duty to deliver them. They did them on a tight budget, within a very short time, without any kind of template."

"I was ecstatic with the webisodes," Rose agrees. "When you think about what went into them and what we did, I think they're amazing. They turned out great."

"The webisodes were one of the most fulfilling assignments Brad and I have had on *Battlestar* because we were asked to step up to the plate with very little lead time, and were given almost complete creative freedom by Ron Moore, David Eick and Sci Fi," Weddle states. "It also made us feel like pioneers, in a way, of a whole new aspect to television drama. We can foresee a time when all shows will have webisodes that add layers of dimension and subplots to the main storyline of the series, making the narrative tapestry infinitely more rich and complex." ■

[SEASON THREE]

The Cylons were created by Man.

They rebelled.

They evolved.

They look and feel Human.

Some are programmed to think they are Human.

There are many copies...

And they have a plan.

THE CAST

Admiral William 'Husker' Adama: Edward James Olmos
President Laura Roslin: Mary McDonnell
Major Lee 'Apollo' Adama: Jamie Bamber (1/2-15, 17-20)
Lt Kara 'Starbuck' Thrace: Katee Sackhoff (1/2-17, 20)
Dr Gaius Baltar: James Callis (1/2-14, 16, 18-20)
Number Six: Tricia Helfer (1/2-8, 10-14, 16, 18-20)
Lt Sharon 'Athena' Agathon/Number Eight: Grace Park
(1/2-15, 17-20)
Colonel Saul Tigh: Michael Hogan (1/2-6, 8-20)
Chief Galen Tyrol: Aaron Douglas
Captain Karl 'Helo' Agathon: Tahmoh Penikett (1/2-12, 14-15, 17-20)
Lt (Junior Grade) Anastasia Dualla: Kandyse McClure
(1/2-5, 7-15, 17-20)
Lt Felix Gaeta: Alessandro Juliani (1/2-15, 17-20)
Cally Henderson-Tyrol: Nicki Clyne (1/2-6, 9, 11-12, 14-16, 18-20)
Ensign Samuel T. Anders: Michael Trucco (1/2-5, 9, 11-13, 17-20)
Tory Foster: Rekha Sharma (1/2, 4-5, 8, 14, 16, 18-20)
Dr Cottle: Donnelly Rhodes (1/2-3, 7-10, 13-14, 20)

THE CREW

Developed by: Ronald D. Moore
Executive Producers: Ronald D. Moore and David Eick
Co-Executive Producers: Mark Verheiden and Michael Angeli
Supervising Producers: Harvey Frand and Michael Taylor
Producers: Bradley Thompson, David Weddle and Michael Rymer
Story Editor: Anne Cofell Saunders
Consulting Producer: Glen A. Larson
Based on the series _Battlestar Galactica_
created by: Glen A. Larson
Production Designer: Richard Hudolin
Art Director: Douglas McLean
Visual Effects Supervisor: Gary Hutzel
Costume Designer: Glenne Campbell
Music: Bear McCreary

[OCCUPATION & PRECIPICE]

WRITER: Ronald D. Moore
DIRECTOR: Sergio Mimica-Gezzan

GUEST CAST: Kate Vernon (Ellen Tigh), Lucy Lawless (D'Anna Biers), Callum Keith Rennie (Leoben Conoy), Dean Stockwell (Brother Cavil), Christian Tessier (Tucker 'Duck' Clellan), Dominic Zamprogna (James 'Jammer' Lyman), Rick Worthy (Simon), Matthew Bennett (Aaron Doral), Richard Hatch (Tom Zarek), Luciana Carro (Captain Louanne 'Kat' Katraine), Madeline Parker (Kacey), Maya (Erica Cerra)

"He's a soldier, Chief. It's not the first time we've sent a soldier on a one-way mission..." — Saul Tigh

Four months into the Cylon occupation of New Caprica, Ellen Tigh secures the release of her husband — by collaborating with the Cylons and sleeping with Brother Cavil. Saul Tigh immediately resumes his role as leader of the Resistance movement, and sees an opportunity to strike a major blow against the Cylons by authorizing Tucker 'Duck' Clellan's suicide bombing of a New Caprica Police graduation ceremony.

In the wake of the bombing, the Cylons force President Baltar to order the summary execution of 200 suspected Resistance sympathizers, including Laura Roslin, Tom Zarek and Cally Henderson-Tyrol. As the prisoners prepare to meet their fate, Leoben continues to hold Kara Thrace captive in a mock domestic setting. Kara's captivity takes an unexpected twist when the Cylon introduces her to a young girl whom he claims is their daughter, Kacey.

Far away from New Caprica, Admiral Adama clashes with his son Lee over his plans to rescue the Colonists. After Lee warns him that a failed rescue attempt could result in the annihilation of the human race, Adama decides the *Galactica* will mount the mission alone while the *Pegasus* stays in deep space to guard the remaining ships of the fleet. Realizing that the Cylon Centurions cannot distinguish between different models of humanoid Cylons, Adama also appoints Sharon Agathon as a Colonial officer and orders her to meet with the Resistance on New Caprica. But shortly after her arrival on the planet, Sharon finds herself under attack with a group of Resistance fighters including Samuel T. Anders...

From the moment the Centurions arrived on New Caprica at the end of season two, Ronald D. Moore was keen to explore what life would be like during a Cylon occupation. "I was really interested to find out what our characters would do in that situation," says Moore, who personally scripted 'Occupation' and 'Precipice' after developing the episodes' storylines with the series' writing staff. "I wanted to take that setting and explore

how the likes of Tyrol, Tigh, Anders and Laura would deal with it.

"A lot of people have asked me if the Cylon occupation was our way of address-ing the situation in Iraq, but it really wasn't," he reveals. "There are obvious parallels, but the truth is when we talked about the episodes in the writers' room, we talked more about Vichy France, Vietnam, the West Bank and various other occupations; we even talked about what happened when the Romans were occupying Gaul. We dis-cussed a lot of different historical examples."

One of Moore's earliest decisions about the season première was that it would open some four months into the Cylon occupation of New Caprica. "I wasn't interested in showing the first few weeks of the occupation, with the Cylons setting everything up and making promises," he explains. "I wanted to jump forward in the narrative, to a time where there was a full-blown insurgency and the story is about to reach a turning point — a point where the Resistance aren't just fighting back but they're taking the gloves off and are going to do everything they can against the Cylons."

That turning point was provided by the Resistance's first suicide bombing. Ironically, this was a late addition to the storyline, as 'Occupation' and 'Precipice' were initially going to focus on the Resistance kidnapping Cylons and keeping them captive.

"In early drafts of the scripts, the Cylons were getting freaked out by the fact that

Above: Ronald D. Moore gave Tigh a lasting injury at the start of season three, to illus-trate the true horror of the Cylon occupation of New Caprica.

their people were disappearing and not downloading," Moore confirms. "The original plot was also much more about the search for Hera. But as I was writing the first episode, I came up with the idea of a suicide bombing and I realized just how powerful and potent and contemporary that would be.

"Once we got into the idea of Duck becoming a suicide bomber, I knew I wanted to do the other side of that and show another of our characters joining the New Caprica Police," he continues. "I wanted to explore the other side of the situation, through Jammer. I thought it was important to show that some of the guys who joined the New Caprica Police did it because they genuinely wanted to help their own people — they figure it's better they police their people rather than the occupying force — and I wanted to show how someone like Jammer could get sucked into that and suddenly find himself on the wrong end of the insurgency."

Another late addition to the season première's storyline was Tigh's loss of an eye during his captivity. Like the suicide bombings, this wasn't in the initial outline of the episodes. "As I was writing the scripts, I realized we needed to find a way to dramatize just how bad the Cylon occupation had been and show that someone had suffered," Moore explains. "I knew Tigh was the leader of the Resistance, so I thought of various injuries he could have sustained — like a bullet wound — and then settled on him losing an eye. I thought that would be a powerful reminder of how people suffered on New Caprica that we could carry on through the series."

Viewers were initially set to see Tigh lose his eye, in a flashback scene. But this sequence was ultimately dropped in favour of Tigh's verbal recollection of the horrific event. "We did shoot the scene, but it just didn't work," reveals David Eick. "We took a very stylized, violent, weird kind of approach to it. It was a point of view shot, with Doral jabbing the lens with a hot poker as Tigh remembered the minute it happened to him.

"The scene was a bit too out of style from the show. I don't think it was in the director's cut, let alone our final cut. We realized that it was far more unsettling for the viewer to simply imagine what the Cylons had done than to actually see it."

Unlike other aspects of the season première, the storyline involving Kara's imprisonment by Leoben remained constant. "That was an idea David Eick and I discussed at the end of season two," Moore recalls. "We actually talked about putting it into the season two finale, but it didn't fit into the structure of that episode. So we kept it for season three."

Kara's 'daughter', Kacey, was named after the niece of producer David Weddle, who suggested the moniker to Moore. Her introduction

SURVEILLANCE: ADDITIONAL

As initially scripted and shot, 'Occupation' and 'Precipice' were two separate episodes. 'Occupation' ended with Duck's suicide bombing and Leoben's introduction of Kacey to Kara, while 'Precipice' opened with an imprisoned Laura Roslin being questioned by Baltar. In post-production, however, the episodes were united to become a movie-length season première.

"We had always told the network we planned to wrap the New Caprica storyline in three weeks," Ronald D. Moore explains. "So when the third part of the storyline — 'Exodus' — became two episodes, we came up with the idea of merging 'Occupation' and 'Precipice' into a two-hour opener. I though that worked well, because 'Occupation' and 'Precipice' had been written and shot simultaneously and were always very interrelated."

allowed Moore to follow-up a plot thread from *Battlestar Galactica*'s previous season. "After we did 'The Farm', everyone kept asking if the Cylons had harvested Kara's ovaries," Moore explains. "So we came up with the idea of doing this storyline."

With Michael Rymer unavailable to work on the season's opening episodes, Moore and Eick enlisted Sergio Mimica-Gezzan to direct 'Occupation' and 'Precipice'. Mimica-Gezzan had firmly established himself as one of *Battlestar Galactica*'s principal directors thanks to his sterling work on 'You Can't Go Home Again', 'Fragged', 'Home, Part I' and 'The Captain's Hand'.

"Sergio's work on the opening episodes was really a unique achievement, because it was the first time anyone other than Michael Rymer had done a première or a finale for us," Eick notes. "We felt Sergio was ready to step up and he completely rose to the occasion. He brought a lot to those episodes."

One of Mimica-Gezzan's most distinctive contributions to the première was the use of night vision to depict the New Caprica Police's capture of Cally Henderson-Tyrol and other Resistance members. "I thought that was a fantastic idea," says Moore. "It really brings a sense of realism to those sequences."

Above: Kara Thrace's imprisonment by Leoben was a story idea that was originally discussed during the development of the season two cliffhanger.

"That was a really cool sequence to shoot," adds Nicki Clyne. "There was hardly any acting involved, because it was really frightening! All these guys wearing masks burst in and shoved us into trucks — it was very believable. It was really neat to play that and the feeling of pure hysteria that Cally feels when she's taken away from her son."

Clyne wasn't alone in enjoying the challenges presented by the season première. During the making of 'Occupation' and 'Precipice', *Battlestar Galactica*'s cast and crew all enjoyed exploring the issues raised by the storyline.

"I loved those episodes because they were so complex and upsetting," explains Mary McDonnell. "It forced you, as an actor, to imagine what it's like to be occupied and really dig your heels in and sit in the mess we created in Iraq. So I found it wonderfully upsetting to play. It was tricky to navigate as a character, because on the one hand Laura supports the insurgency 100 per cent because there's nothing else to be done in order to survive, but on the other hand, she cannot agree with suicide bombings. It was very interesting."

"I thought that storyline was fantastic and it turned out really well," Aaron Douglas agrees. "It was a timeless statement on humanity — on how people respond to being invaded."

"I love the complicated picture the première paints," Moore adds. "I love that Tigh is very open about the fact that what the Resistance is doing is wrong. I love the scene between Baltar and Laura, for the way it challenges the audience's loyalties and whose side we should be on. That's probably my favourite scene in the première. And I also love the fact that Jammer is ultimately the person who saves Cally. How does that affect the way you feel about him — the collaborator?"

Moral complexity is also at the heart of Ellen Tigh's new relationship with Brother Cavil. This is established by some shocking glimpses of Ellen having sex with the Cylon during the première's opening moments. "Those shots were extremely raunchy," says Kate Vernon of the Ellen/Cavil sex scene. "It's not about love-making, beauty or any kind of a connection. It's more violent. Ellen wants to kill this man. She wants to break him in half in that scene.

"It was a fun scene to shoot," she laughs. "That was my first scene with Dean Stockwell. We met and within a few minutes, Dean was lying down and he looked at me and said, 'Are you ready, kid?' I said 'Yeah, let's go!' It was funny."

Cavil's references to Ellen's 'twist' and 'swirl' were a nod to the *Seinfeld* episode 'The Fusilli Jerry'. "I am a complete *Seinfeld* nut," Moore explains. "So I'm very proud to say the 'twist' and the 'swirl' is a complete homage to that show."

In addition to featuring the return of Brother Cavil, 'Occupation' and 'Precipice' brings Number Three — a.k.a. D'Anna Biers — into the series on a recurring basis. "I was very happy to come back," says Lucy Lawless of her return to *Battlestar Galactica*. "It's a great show, brilliantly written, and I loved the idea of doing a really exciting, compact storyline over a series of episodes, rather than appear briefly in a few episodes here and there."

One plotline that Moore never considered exploring with D'Anna, however, was her exposure as a Cylon. "I felt there wasn't anything to mine there," he says. "So I thought, 'Let's move on.' Somewhere along the line, she's been found out and everyone now knows she's a Cylon. I thought that was all the viewer needs to know."

The season première concludes with Roslin, Cally Henderson-Tyrol, Tom Zarek and other Resistance sympathizers facing execution, in a scenario inspired by the climax of the classic 1963 war film *The Great Escape*. As conceived by Moore, the scene also allows Roslin and Zarek to enjoy a rare moment of rapport.

"I thought that was very interesting," says McDonnell. "It was wonderful to see these political foes suddenly finding themselves together as potential victims, and explore how that changes their chemistry. The person you thought was your enemy becomes your friend.

"Of course, that didn't last long," she adds with a laugh. "Nothing lasts that long in *Battlestar Galactica*!"

Following principal photography on the season première, Eick and Moore ordered the recording of an opening narration by Laura Roslin, which they felt would allow new viewers to follow the show. While Eick favoured the narration being placed right at the start of the episode, he was ultimately persuaded to move it to the second act by Moore. Another point of contention between the makers of the series concerned the placing of the first scene aboard the *Galactica*, with Moore resisting calls for viewers to return to the Battlestar before the third act.

"I liked the idea of viewers having to wait for the first *Galactica* scene, so that they're really excited when it finally comes," Moore explains. "The *Galactica* and *Pegasus* storyline of the opening episodes stayed pretty much the same from the beginning. We wanted to set up the idea they are planning to return to New Caprica, we wanted to establish Sharon's new relationship with Adama and we wanted to continue to play 'Fat Lee', which was a metaphor for the fact that the fleet has gone soft. The only thing we ever really debated was just how much of a hard time Adama would give Lee."

By the time the episodes were completed, everyone involved with *Battlestar Galactica* felt that 'Occupation' and 'Precipice' had emerged as a truly outstanding start to season three. "Through a lot of hard work and healthy debate we arrived at an incredibly powerful and intensely memorable première," says Eick. "It is definitely in the cannon of 'best-ever *Battlestar Galactica*'."

"I'm very happy with the third-season première," Moore agrees. "I think it's among the best things we've done." ■

Above: The season première establishes Sharon Agathon's new relationship with Admiral Adama.

WRITERS: Bradley Thompson & David Weddle
DIRECTOR: Felix Alcala

GUEST CAST: Kate Vernon (Ellen Tigh), Richard Hatch (Tom Zarek), Lucy Lawless (D'Anna Biers), Matthew Bennett (Aaron Doral), Callum Keith Rennie (Leoben Conoy), Dean Stockwell (Brother Cavil), Amanda Plummer (Oracle Selloi), Maya (Erica Cerra), Madeline Parker (Kacey), Luciana Carro (Captain Louanne 'Kat' Katraine), Leah Cairns (Lieutenant Margaret 'Racetrack' Edmondson), Jennifer Halley (Seelix), Dominic Zamprogna (James 'Jammer' Lyman), Eileen Pedde (Gunnery Sergeant Mathias), Ryan Robbins (Charlie Connor)

"This is the Admiral. You've heard the news. You know the mission. You should also know that there is only one way that this mission ends — and that's with the successful rescue of our people off of New Caprica..." — Admiral William Adama

---

Learning of Cally's planned execution with the other Resistance sympathizers, Tyrol quickly forms a rescue team. With just seconds to spare, Tyrol's unit attacks and destroys a firing squad of Cylon Centurions before they can execute their prisoners.

Meanwhile, after narrowly surviving an ambush, Anders realizes that Ellen Tigh must have betrayed the Resistance by providing the Cylons with information about their rendezvous with Sharon Agathon. As Anders tells Saul Tigh of his wife's actions, Sharon successfully enters the Cylon detention centre and steals the launch keys that will allow the fleet ships to escape New Caprica. Before she leaves the centre Sharon encounters D'Anna Biers, who tries to test the Colonial officer's loyalty by telling her she believes her daughter, Hera, is alive.

When Admiral Adama learns that Sharon has successfully retrieved the launch keys, he orders the *Galactica* to Jump to New Caprica and initiates the rescue plan...

SURVEILLANCE: ADDITIONAL

Chief Tyrol and Cally's son was named by David Weddle. "David named Nick after his maternal grandfather, an Irish farmer who came to Irvington, New York and worked on the big estates there," explains Bradley Thompson.

Before season three had even entered pre-production, it was a given that the Colonial survivors would somehow escape Cylon-occupied New Caprica and resume their quest for Earth. The task of actually hatching the escape plan fell not on William Adama or Laura Roslin but on *Battlestar Galactica*'s resident military experts, David Weddle and Bradley Thompson.

"Ron Moore and David Eick tend to throw us the big battle shows because Brad has an encyclopedic knowledge of warfare, both on an infantry level and in air and sea combat, which is somewhat analogous to space battles," Weddle notes. "And because my father was a marine in World War II, I have a feel for the psychology

Above: Lee Adama bids farewell to his father.

of soldiers and combat veterans."

"The writing staff had already outlined the first two episodes that Ron was scripting when we started working on 'Exodus'," Thompson continues. "So we had to pick up from them and get them off the planet in one episode — that was the brief."

Drawing on their proven knowledge of military history and psychology, Thompson and Weddle discussed several possible escape plans with the writing staff before settling on the final version that would feature in the series. One early attack strategy involved the *Galactica* faking its destruction and posing as the *Pegasus*.

"In early drafts, *Galactica* had worked out a procedure for Jumping during a simulated runaway Tylium detonation," Thompson explains. "The plan was for the *Galactica* to come in, take the heat off the Colony and — when hit by the Cylon nukes — set up the phony detonation and Jump away under the cover of the flash of one of her own nukes. The *Galactica* would then arrive halfway around the planet, pretending to be the *Pegasus*, and pull the Cylons over there long enough for the Colonists to escape. The *Galactica* was then going to get thrashed and at the last

SURVEILLANCE: ADDITIONAL

'Exodus, Part I' introduces Ryan Robbins as Resistance member (and future bartender) Charlie Connor. Robbins previously played the doomed Armistice Station Officer in the opening scene of the *Battlestar Galactica* miniseries.

moment, Lee would save Adama with *Pegasus*' surprise '*Millennium Falcon* arrival'.

"Unfortunately, that was too unwieldy and rough to comprehend," Thompson says of this plan, "so Ron simplified it on his pass."

As the escape from New Caprica took shape, the writers toyed with killing off various characters. These briefly included none other than the *Pegasus*' Executive Officer, Anastasia Dualla, and — far less surprisingly — the doomed collaborator Jammer. "In early drafts of the script, Jammer died in the firefight at the start of the episode," Ron Moore confirms. "But ultimately we decided to move his death back to 'Collaborators', which we felt had greater dramatic potential."

Although it was initially planned, scripted and shot as a single episode, the show's producers decided to rework 'Exodus' into a two-part adventure when the episode entered post-production. "I think we all sensed 'Exodus' was going to be a two-parter from quite early on," Moore notes. "We just knew that to play the action beats correctly and deal with all the various plot threads that were coming together, we couldn't do it in an hour. The episode's midway point — Adama's speech — also lent itself nicely to ending an episode, so it was a good creative decision. It helped us financially too, because the episodes on New Caprica had been really expensive and we could save money by splitting one episode into two."

By the time 'Exodus' officially became two episodes, Thompson and Weddle were hard at work on the script for 'Rapture'. This led to Moore enlisting Michael Angeli to script some additional scenes for the expanded tale. Angeli's main additions were the farewell between the crews of the *Pegasus* and the *Galactica* in Part I and Part II's opening discussion between Lee and Dualla. "Michael wrote some wonderful scenes with tremendous heart," says Weddle of Angeli's work on 'Exodus'. "We really appreciate the contribution Michael made to the episodes."

'Exodus' marked Felix Alcala's first foray into the *Battlestar Galactica* universe. A veteran TV director whose many credits include episodes of *ER*, *NYPD Blue* and *The Shield*, Alcala was picked to helm 'Exodus' by Moore.

"Felix was going to direct my *Dragonriders of Pern* pilot that was abandoned by the WB, so I knew him from that," Moore reveals. "We were all aware that 'Exodus' was going to be very complicated to do, and I knew Felix would do a great job bringing it in."

In addition to setting up the escape attempt and continuing the Kara/Leoben plotline, 'Exodus, Part I' begins D'Anna Biers' arc for the season with her visit to the Oracle. This Moore-scripted scene was originally written and shot as part of the teaser for 'Occupation' and features the Oracle Dodona Selloi (whom Moore named after an oracle from ancient Greece). Selloi is played by Emmy Award-winning actress Amanda Plummer, whose many screen credits include *Law & Order: Special Victims Unit*, *Pulp Fiction*, *The Fisher King* and *The Outer Limits*.

"That was a great piece of casting," says Moore. "Amanda Plummer is one of my favourite actresses and it was great to have her on the show."

The latter half of 'Exodus, Part I' features several homages to war and action movies. D'Anna's objection to Sharon Agathon's decision to give her word to Admiral Adama was inspired by Ernest Borgnine's famous exchange with William Holden in *The Wild Bunch*, while Sharon shooting D'Anna in the leg is a nod to *Terminator 2: Judgment Day*. Similarly, the episode's closing moments took their cues from *The Longest Day* and Shakespeare's *Henry V*.

"I wanted the show to be a little bit less natural and more classic in that scene," says Moore of Adama's climactic speech. "So it's a *Henry V* moment with Adama talking to his crew. It provides us with a really good set-up for the next episode." ∎

Below: Admiral Adama's climactic speech to his crew was devised by Moore and writers David Weddle and Bradley Thompson as a "*Henry V* moment".

[EXODUS, PART II]

WRITERS: Bradley Thompson & David Weddle
DIRECTOR: Felix Alcala

GUEST CAST: Kate Vernon (Ellen Tigh), Richard Hatch (Tom Zarek), Callum Keith Rennie (Leoben Conoy), Lucy Lawless (D'Anna Biers), Matthew Bennett (Aaron Doral), Rick Worthy (Simon), Dominic Zamprogna (James 'Jammer' Lyman), Luciana Carro (Captain Louanne 'Kat' Katraine), Ryan Robbins (Charlie Connor), Ty Olsson (Captain Kelly), Eileen Pedde (Gunnery Sergeant Mathias), Madeline Parker (Kacey Brynn), Emilie Ullerup (Julia Brynn), Leah Cairns (Lieutenant Margaret 'Racetrack' Edmondson), Bodie Olmos (Lieutenant Brenden 'Hotdog' Costanza)

"You did it. You brought them home, Saul." — Admiral Adama
"Not all of them..." — Saul Tigh

Faced with details of Ellen's collaboration with the Cylons, Saul Tigh confronts his wife about her betrayal of the Resistance. After Ellen tells him she collaborated simply to save his life, Tigh knows she must die for her crime and watches as his wife drinks a fatal dose of poison.

While the Resistance begins a coordinated ground attack on Cylon forces, the Cylons detect the *Galactica* and the *Pegasus* in orbit of the planet. By the time the Cylons realize that the *Galactica* is alone (and using drones to simulate the *Pegasus*' presence), the *Galactica* is able to Jump into the atmosphere of New Caprica and launch its Vipers. The daring move enables the Vipers to aid the exodus of Colonial ships from the planet.

Following its Jump into New Caprica's atmosphere, the battle-damaged *Galactica* is an easy target for the four Cylon Basestars orbiting the planet. But before the Cylons can destroy the *Galactica*, the Battlestar *Pegasus* comes to its rescue on a suicide mission.

As the escape from New Caprica continues, Gaeta moves to kill Baltar. On hearing that the Cylons are planning to destroy the Colony with a bomb, he spares the President's life in return for Baltar's promise to stop D'Anna. Baltar's chance discovery of Hera convinces D'Anna against her deadly plan and leads to him escaping the planet with the Cylons.

On the *Galactica*, Adama is hailed as a hero by the survivors of the exodus. But the celebratory mood is not felt by Tigh or Kara Thrace. As Tigh faces the loss of his wife, Kara has to grapple with the discovery that Kacey wasn't her daughter at all...

SURVEILLANCE: ADDITIONAL

'Exodus, Part II' won the 2007 Visual Effects Society Award for Outstanding Visual Effects in a Broadcast Series. The award was presented at the VES Fifth Annual Awards ceremony in February 2007.

The death of Ellen Tigh was one of the first story ideas that *Battlestar Galactica*'s writing staff agreed on during the development of season three. "We started talking about the idea that Ellen would collaborate with the Cylons to save Tigh, and that she would have to pay the price for that — at her husband's hands," Ronald D. Moore recalls. "We always knew it was going to be a really great and powerful storyline that would take both Ellen and Tigh to an interesting place."

"The decision to have Ellen pass information to the Cylons came to us pretty early in the outlining process," David Weddle continues. "We knew it fit into the tragic pattern of her relationship with Tigh and never considered any other options. There was some debate over the method of her execution. I advocated having Tigh shoot her, but then Mark Verheiden came up with the idea to poison her. That was a stroke of genius."

As soon as the details of Ellen Tigh's fate had been finalized, Moore and David Eick told Kate Vernon of her character's impending demise. "I had called Ron and David about my scene with Dean Stockwell in the première," Vernon recalls. "I told them how I wanted to play it and they were happy to accommodate all my ideas. I said, 'You guys are wonderful! You're the best producers in the world. I love working with you.' There was then this awkward silence, followed by one of them saying, 'Let's talk about the arc of your character...' They went on to tell me how much they loved what I'd done with the role — which really worried me — and then said they had to kill me off in 'Exodus'!

Above: 'Exodus, Part II' resolves the Kacey storyline with the revelation she is not really Kara Thrace's daughter.

"I was just stunned and devastated by the news," she admits. "It was hard to hear. I loved working on the show. But from a dramatic point of view, I thought it was brilliant because what happens to Ellen is so tragic and unfair and unjust. She risks her life to save her husband, using the only skills she has: her feminine wiles. And the tragedy is that she is finally able to show she loves her husband and is willing to do anything for him — and she gets killed for that!"

"It was heart-wrenching to tell Kate about Ellen's death," says Moore. "It was hard for everyone, because we all love Kate and what she did with Ellen. But we knew the storyline would be really powerful for the series."

Moore's views on Ellen Tigh's demise are echoed by Michael Hogan. "It was a very clever position to put Tigh in," he notes. "When he finds out what Ellen has done, he has no choice. As an actor, it was rewarding to do that storyline and I thought the way Kate played it was amazing. But it was also horrible to lose Kate."

Following the death of Ellen Tigh, 'Exodus, Part II' is then driven by the escape from New Caprica, in what Moore describes as "one of the biggest and most sustained action sequences we've done on the series." The start of the mission is heralded by the *Galactica*'s brief FTL Jump into New Caprica's sky, a moment Moore added to the script. "Ron felt the battle needed something spectacular that we'd never seen before — a jaw dropper," Weddle explains. "And he more than delivered it."

"There was something really delicious about the idea of the *Galactica* Jumping into the atmosphere," Moore says. "We had some internal questions about the technical feasibility of a Battlestar doing that, but ultimately it's science fiction so we just did it. And I love it — it's a beautiful moment."

Throughout the development of 'Exodus', the escape from New Caprica was always set to culminate in the destruction of the Battlestar *Pegasus*. "I thought it was interesting to keep the *Pegasus* around for a while, but there was something pure about the *Galactica* being the last Battlestar," says Moore of the *Pegasus*' demise. "There were also practical reasons for doing it — the *Pegasus* sets were eating up a soundstage and we needed the space for the Cylon Basestar sets."

The actual depiction of the *Pegasus*' destruction required a visual effects *tour de force* from Gary Hutzel and his team, who greatly embellished the script's description of the Battlestar's final assault on the Cylons. "We worked hard to make the idea of the *Pegasus* ramming a Cylon Basestar seem believable," Hutzel recalls. "We also came up with the idea of the *Pegasus*' pod flying off into a second Basestar in pre-viz. That's something we normally wouldn't do — it's not in our usual house style — but when I showed it to Michael Rymer and asked if he felt we'd gone too far, he said, 'No, that's perfect. You should do that.' So we did."

"We wrote the destruction of *Pegasus*, but did not appreciate the full power of it until we saw the way Gary Hutzel's team brought it to fruition," says Weddle. "When I saw the nameplate of the destroyed *Pegasus* fly toward camera I got tears in my eyes. I didn't think it was possible to cry over a visual effect, but Gary proved me wrong!"

Directly before the *Pegasus*' demise, Admiral Adama finds himself nobly facing his own death in what Moore feels is a "key moment" that distinguishes the character from larger-than-life, 'never-say-die'-type TV heroes. Adama also finds himself in the thick of the action with the rest of the *Galactica*'s crew, including the Battlestar's acting Executive Officer, Karl 'Helo' Agathon. "Those scenes took a lot of time to do, but they were huge fun," says Tahmoh Penikett. "Eddie really kept the energy up on set. He did his own stunts — he was throwing himself around and jumping on stuff. We all got a kick out of that."

During the final moments of the escape from New Caprica, Gaeta threatens to kill Baltar in a scene Weddle and Thompson conceived while writing their script. Kara's captivity is also ended in a manner that deliberately leaves her state of mind open to

debate. "You're left wondering if Kara has been broken by Leoben," Moore points out. "I thought that was an interesting question for viewers to ponder."

Something that isn't left open to question, however, is Kara's relationship with her 'daughter', Kacey. 'Exodus, Part II' resolves that storyline, in a manner casually suggested by Anne Cofell Saunders. "We were all throwing out ideas about how we could resolve Kara's storyline with Kacey and I quipped that a woman could just walk up and thank Kara for saving her baby," Cofell Saunders recalls. "It stuck and made it to the final version."

The resolution of the Kara/Kacey storyline forms part of the celebration scene on the *Galactica*'s hangar deck. "Felix Alcala did a masterful job of choreographing that scene on the hangar deck where Adama is hoisted on to the crowd's shoulders while Tigh and Kara baste in their personal hells," says Weddle. "It was a powerful and poetic blend of conflicting and converging emotions and it never fails to bring tears to my eyes when I watch it."

'Exodus, Part II' concludes with Admiral Adama shaving his moustache, in a scene that symbolizes the conclusion of the New Caprica storyline. It also provides a touching end to one of *Battlestar Galactica*'s most thrilling adventures.

"'Exodus' is just a rocket ride from beginning to end," says David Eick. "It's quite something to watch, both visually and in terms of its intensity, pace and visual effects. I'd put it alongside our best episodes."

"Bradley and I are enormously proud of the 'Exodus' episodes," Weddle declares. "It was thrilling to participate in the climax of the New Caprica storyline, which I think is some of the best work we've ever done." ∎

Above: The evocative celebration scene in 'Exodus, Part II' deliberately mixes conflicting feelings of triumph and tragedy.

[COLLABORATORS]

WRITER: Mark Verheiden
DIRECTOR: Michael Rymer

GUEST CAST: Richard Hatch (Tom Zarek), Lucy Lawless (D'Anna Biers), Dominic Zamprogna (James 'Jammer' Lyman), Jennifer Halley (Seelix), Ryan Robbins (Charlie Connor), Alisen Down (Jean Barolay), Priest (Winston Rekert)

"The whole thing is like a bad dream: we woke up and the traitors are still here..." — Kara Thrace

Following the escape from New Caprica, a secret group known as the Circle is passing judgment on people suspected of collaborating with the Cylons — and executing those found guilty. Sanctioned by acting President Tom Zarek, the group's members include Saul Tigh, Galen Tyrol and Samuel T. Anders.

After the execution of former New Caprica Police officer James 'Jammer' Lyman, the Circle turns its attention to Felix Gaeta. Just before Gaeta is executed, however, Tyrol realizes that Baltar's former aide had secretly been supplying the Resistance with information.

On replacing Zarek as President of the Twelve Colonies, Laura Roslin immediately ends the Circle's activities. Instead, she issues a general pardon for suspected collaborators and forms a Commission for Truth and Reconciliation.

Far away from the fleet, Gaius Baltar finds himself imprisoned on a Cylon Basestar. D'Anna tells him the Cylons are debating his value to them — and his fate...

Opposite: Even Alessandro Juliani was worried for Felix Gaeta's future when he learned his character would be facing execution in 'Collaborators'.

The premise of 'Collaborators' developed naturally from events in the opening episodes of *Battlestar Galactica*'s third season. "During our initial discussions about season three, one of the first things we asked ourselves was, 'What happens when everyone gets back on the ship?'" explains Ronald D. Moore. "We needed to explore what would happen when those who collaborated with the Cylons were back on the ship, rubbing shoulders with those who fought the Cylons on New Caprica.

"We talked about what had happened in France after the Nazis had been driven out and how there had been a brief time where people were settling scores. And it seemed to us that something very similar would happen on the *Galactica* too."

'Collaborators' was destined to be a particularly difficult episode to script. Not only did its main storyline involve some of the darkest and most disturbing ideas of *Battlestar Galactica*'s run, but the episode's B-plot would give viewers their first glimpse of life inside a Cylon Basestar. Fortunately, co-executive producer Mark Verheiden relished the challenges presented by scripting 'Collaborators'.

"I was definitely drawn to this 'aftermath' story, since showing consequences is

Above: 'Collaborators' gives viewers their first glimpse of life inside a Cylon Baseship.

what we do best on *Battlestar Galactica*," Verheiden says. "But it was a struggle to shape the material to find the right balance for the story. When you go this dark, you're really pushing the envelope. There was a very scary component — showing Tigh, Tyrol and Starbuck in a star chamber actually executing a semi-regular was pretty heavy stuff, and there were concerns that it would be difficult to redeem the characters after that.

"It was equally complicated to land on the Cylon Baseship material. This was the first episode to go aboard a Baseship and that meant a lot of big decisions had to be made — decisions that would affect future episodes."

While the premise of 'Collaborators' remained constant, the episode's plotline changed significantly during pre-production. Early versions of the story didn't involve the Circle but instead concerned acts of retribution carried out by vigilantes. These acts were sanctioned by President Zarek, who later issued the call for reconciliation, as well as a blanket pardon, before handing over power to Roslin. Tigh also played a less significant role in the hunt for the collaborators in early drafts, and at one point was actually going to be responsible for saving Gaeta.

On receiving the completed script for 'Collaborators', director Michael Rymer felt that he couldn't have wished for a better episode to mark his return to *Battlestar Galactica*. "I was so happy to get 'Collaborators' as my first episode of season three — it was a great script that was very much about character and performance, which are my favourite aspects of the process," he explains. "It was also really satisfying to give certain actors, like Alessandro Juliani and Aaron Douglas, so much screen time."

Rymer's excitement about working on 'Collaborators' was shared by Juliani, who was thrilled by Gaeta's pivotal role in the episode. But on his initial read-through of the script, he did become concerned that the producers had forgotten to tell him something.

"When I first read the script I remember thinking about halfway through, 'This is looking a bit dicey for Felix. I haven't been told I'm not coming back, but maybe they forgot to tell me…'" Juliani recalls with a laugh. "Then I got to the scene where they apprehend Gaeta, put the hood on his head and condemn him to death, and the script cut to another scene. I remember having a moment of panic and flipping to the end of the script to see if Gaeta was still alive! I was relieved to see he was.

"Making that episode was one of my highlights of doing the series so far," he continues. "I really got to flex my muscles as an actor. I remember the afternoon we shot the scene where the Circle tries to kill Gaeta. The tone on set was very different. There wasn't the usual banter between takes; everyone was pretty respectful of the gravity of the situation and the intensity of what was needed from the actors to pull that off."

During the shooting of the Circle's attempted execution of Gaeta, Juliani decided that his character shouldn't beg for his life (as originally planned), but instead should realize the futility of his situation. "I thought that was a really smart decision," Moore notes. "It makes that scene even more interesting."

As one of Gaeta's would-be executioners, Aaron Douglas was concerned about his character's involvement with the Circle. "I didn't want the Chief to become fundamentally dark and unlikable," Douglas explains. "So I really tried to concentrate on showing how the Chief was struggling with what the Circle was doing."

Following Gaeta's attempted execution, the episode ends with him sharing a table with Tyrol. "I thought that was a really bittersweet ending," Moore says. "There are no apologies or explanations. Those two characters are just going to keep going."

In addition to its A- and B-plots, 'Collaborators' begins Tigh's struggle to resume his life on the *Galactica* following events on New Caprica. It also features Laura Roslin's re-appointment as President of the Twelve Colonies.

"We knew we wanted Laura to take back the Presidency right from the beginning," Verheiden notes, "but we definitely did not want to do another election story. With Baltar theoretically dead, Zarek would ascend to the Presidency automatically, so finding a way for Zarek to hand over the reins of power without causing a tumult in the fleet was the challenge."

Mary McDonnell appreciated the nature of Roslin's return to power. "One of the things I admire about Laura's Presidency is the lack of fanfare," she explains. "So whenever we do something simple like that, I appreciate it because I feel it keeps the character pure."

In addition to regaining her power, Laura also shares a kiss with Baltar during a 'dream' sequence. That kiss replaced the originally scripted moment in which Laura casually shot the fallen President. "That was something they came up with on set," Moore reports. "It's a fun moment."

Laura's kiss with Baltar was just one of the many things that helped 'Collaborators' emerge as one of the most memorable instalments of *Battlestar Galactica*'s third season. "It turned out to be a powerful episode," Verheiden notes. "It's extremely well acted by all concerned, especially Dominic Zamprogna and Alessandro Juliani. It also goes to all those good places that *Battlestar Galactica* goes, exploring guilt, vengeance and the morality of judging others."

"It's one of my favourite episodes," says Rymer. "It's obviously very dark — in terms of television entertainment, I think we might have gone a little too far, actually. But I also feel it was incredibly truthful about human nature and the long-term damage done by war and oppression to have the characters turn on each other right away. I think that's why *Battlestar* is so strong — we don't shy away from showing these things." ∎

[TORN]

WRITER: Anne Cofell Saunders
DIRECTOR: Jean de Segonzac

GUEST CAST: Lucy Lawless (D'Anna Biers), Callum Keith Rennie (Leoben Conoy), Rick Worthy (Simon), Matthew Bennett (Aaron Doral), Luciana Carro (Captain Louanne 'Kat' Katraine), Tiffany Lyndall-Knight (The Hybrid), Emilie Ullerup (Julia Brynn), Madeline Parker (Kacey Brynn), Bodie Olmos (Lieutenant Brenden 'Hotdog' Costanza), Leah Cairns (Lieutenant Margaret 'Racetrack' Edmondson), Sebastian Spence (Lieutenant Noel 'Narcho' Allison)

> "What's the matter? No guts? You don't got a pair? You're both frakking cowards..."
>
> — William Adama, to Kara Thrace and Saul Tigh

O n the Cylon Basestar, D'Anna and Caprica Six tell Baltar the Cylons are now seeking Earth and ask if he knows the planet's location. In a bid to save his life, Baltar tells them about his research and the Cylons send a Basestar on the course he had been plotting for the *Galactica*.

When the Cylons learn that the Basestar and its inhabitants have been infected with a disease, Baltar attempts to prove his worth to the Cylons by visiting the vessel to investigate. After they discover that a man-made probe is the source of the disease, the Cylons begin to suspect that Baltar set them up.

Back on the *Galactica*, divisions begin to develop between the officers who suffered during the Cylon occupation of New Caprica and those who stayed on the Battlestar. Aware of the damage it is doing to morale, Admiral Adama confronts Saul Tigh and Kara Thrace about their resentful behaviour. Following their heated discussion, Kara recommits herself to military life — but Tigh tells Adama he will not be returning to duty.

As life on the *Galactica* returns to normal, a Raptor scout party arrives at the location of the diseased Cylon Basestar...

The sixth episode of *Battlestar Galactica*'s third season initially began life with a very different storyline from the one it ultimately depicted. "'Torn' was originally going to be about Kara struggling to let go of Kacey when Kacey's mother proves to be less than ideal," explains writer Anne Cofell Saunders, who scripted the episode after developing its storyline with the show's writing staff. "At one point, Kara actually turned in her wings to do right by the little girl — that's where the title 'Torn' first came from.

"But during the script development process, Kara's character seemed too scarred

by her time with Leoben to go on this path. So we moved away from that and the Cylon story became the A-plot. Some of Baltar's first experiences on the Cylon ship, including his first meeting with The Hybrid, were moved from 'Collaborators' to this episode. So 'Torn' became our first window into the Cylon world.

"We kept the title because we thought it worked very well with the B-story in the final version of the script," she adds. "The troops that went down to New Caprica find themselves at odds with the ones that stayed behind — so 'Torn' still seemed an appropriate title to reflect that."

Throughout its development, however, 'Torn' served to pave the way for the next instalment of season three, 'A Measure of Salvation'. "'Torn' is very much a bridge episode," Ronald D. Moore confirms. "It sets up the Cylon virus plotline and follows Baltar's attempts to prove his worth to the Cylons — and how that backfires on him. The episode ends with the two storylines crossing, with the *Galactica* and the Cylons in the same place."

With Baltar's presence on the Cylon Basestar established in 'Collaborators', 'Torn' was required to continue season three's exploration of the Cylon world. While the Cylon Basestar sets had been deliberately designed to depict an "unworldly sci-fi environment", Moore felt it was necessary to emphasise the Basestar's surreal nature through several additional creative choices.

"The problem we had with showing the inside of the Cylon Basestar is that whatever the viewer had imagined was always going to be cooler than what we actually showed," he explains. "So I started to play the idea of it being an odd, offbeat environment by doing things like using dissolving images and multiple takes. The

Above: Kara Thrace struggles to adapt back into life on the *Galactica* following her experiences as a prisoner on New Caprica.

SURVEILLANCE: ADDITIONAL

'Torn' marked Jean de Segonzac's first foray into the *Battlestar Galactica* universe. The veteran TV director had previously helmed episodes of such shows as *Law & Order, Homicide: Life on the Streets* and *Oz*.

idea of that piano music that plays all the way through, without changing to suit the mood of the scene, also adds to that strange out-of-body quality.

"The use of Cylon projection was another way to make life on the Basestar interesting," he adds. "I didn't want the audience to be disappointed by the characters walking by all these walls and lights, so I figured Cylons could choose to envision their surroundings in any way they like."

During his initial tour of the Basestar, Baltar encounters a Sharon who is practising tai chi — naked. While the scene serves to underline the Cylons' sensuality and lack of a need for privacy, it also required Grace Park to film another nude scene. "I didn't really mind doing it," Park recalls. "But I think it would have been more interesting if we had had Simon or Leoben doing naked tai chi!"

'Torn' also introduces The Cylon Hybrid, played by prolific theatre actress and TV guest star Tiffany Lyndall-Knight (whose many credits include roles in *Da Vinci's City Hall, Supernatural, Smallville* and *Stargate SG-1*). These scenes were actually all re-shot following principal photography on the episode. "The first time we did it, it didn't work," Moore explains. "The Hybrid didn't have the pale look on her face and was just too aware of her environment, so I said we needed to re-do it."

The episode's B-plot sees Kara and Tigh causing dissent in the ranks as a result of their experiences on New Caprica. This culminates in an electrifying confrontation between Adama, Kara and Tigh. "That's probably my favourite scene in the episode," Moore says. "It's Eddie at his best."

Kara responds to Adama's complaint by recommitting herself to military life, which is symbolized by her decision to cut her hair. The shooting of Kara's hair-cutting scene saw Katee Sackhoff cutting off a combination of extensions and her own hair, using a knife. "I really went to town for that scene," Sackhoff reveals. "I actually cut my arm doing it! I have two scars now because the knife was so sharp."

On a less dramatic note, 'Torn' has Sharon Agathon adopting a call sign — Athena. This homage to the character played by Maren Jensen in the original *Battlestar Galactica* was Moore's idea. "I did it on impulse," he explains. "I thought it was another nice bit of continuity to the old show."

During post-production on 'Torn', Moore made several major changes to the episode. The botched Viper pilot exercise was moved from the teaser to the episode's first act, while a scene featuring Baltar and Number Six on the beach was split into two sequences, one of which was used in the episode's new teaser. A substantial amount of dialogue was also changed during editing, to clarify certain story points.

Above: Adama's confrontation with Tigh and Kara is an obvious highlight of 'Torn' for Moore.

"When 'Torn' entered post-production, I was hearing that it was a very troubled episode," Moore explains. "There were some problems with the narrative, so we had to find a way to fix those. I also didn't like the original teaser, so I thought, 'Let's start the episode off with the most provocative image — Tricia Helfer in a red bikini out on the beach.'"

Anne Cofell Saunders credits Moore's editing choices for helping make 'Torn' a fascinating foray into the Cylon Basestar. "'Torn' was the 'new world' episode chocked full of fresh concepts," she notes. "I was riveted by James Callis' performance. It's Baltar's all-too-human reactions that really sell the Cylon ship's alien environment." ∎

SURVEILLANCE: ADDITIONAL ||||

Lee Adama reverts to his familiar look in 'Torn', as the episode reveals that he has lost the weight he gained during the settlement on New Caprica. But the episode's casual solution to Lee's problem was not what Ronald D. Moore had initially envisaged. "We'd originally talked about Lee getting back in shape by joining the marines and becoming a pure spartan warrior," Moore reveals. "But we couldn't get that to work and basically we just went, 'You know what? He's not 'Fat Apollo' any more. He's been working out and he's lost weight. We actually added that scene into 'Torn' to emphasise that idea.

"Frankly, the 'Fat Apollo' storyline wasn't our finest hour," he admits. "It was an interesting idea, but I don't think we knew what to do with it."

[A MEASURE OF SALVATION]

WRITER: Michael Angeli
DIRECTOR: Bill Eagles

GUEST CAST: Lucy Lawless (D'Anna Biers), Callum Keith Rennie (Leoben Conoy), Rick Worthy (Simon), Matthew Bennett (Aaron Doral), Tiffany Lyndall-Knight (The Hybrid), Leah Cairns (Lieutenant Margaret 'Racetrack' Edmondson), Bodie Olmos (Lieutenant Brenden 'Hotdog' Constanza), Eileen Pedde (Gunnery Sergeant Elise Mathias)

"Admiral Adama, as President I have determined the Cylons be made extinct. The use of biological weapons is authorized." — Laura Roslin
"So say we all." — William Adama

After boarding the infected Cylon Basestar, Lee Adama's team returns to the *Galactica* with a group of dying humanoid Cylons. Lee realizes that if the Cylons are executed in the vicinity of a Resurrection Ship, they will download and spread the fatal virus to the rest of the Cylon race. Admiral Adama and Karl 'Helo' Agathon are troubled by the moral questions this plan raises, but President Roslin decides it should be carried out.

As the *Galactica* crew prepares to face the Cylons for one last time, D'Anna Biers accuses Baltar of leading the Cylons to the virus and interrogates him. During his torture, the Number Six that resides in Baltar's mind talks him through the pain and helps him make a connection with D'Anna. Shocked by his ability to endure and his profession of love for her, D'Anna ends Baltar's torture.

The *Galactica* Jumps to known Cylon space and Admiral Adama orders Lee to execute the prisoners. But when Lee's team enters the cell, they discover the Cylons are already dead — due to Helo secretly reversing the air purification system.

Following the *Galactica*'s escape from the Cylons, Admiral Adama tells President Roslin he is relieved they did not commit genocide and informs her they will not investigate Helo's suspected murder of the Cylon prisoners. Adama also reveals that Doc Cottle's research suggests the probe was left behind by the Thirteenth Tribe, which means they are on the right road to Earth — as are the Cylons...

'A Measure of Salvation' was the second episode of *Battlestar Galactica* to be scripted by Michael Angeli, following his work as a freelance writer on the first-season instalment 'Six Degrees of Separation'. "'Measure of Salvation' was very different to my first episode, which was one of the things that excited me about it," Angeli recalls. "'Six Degrees' was designed to be a humorous episode that showed a different side to Baltar, whereas 'A Measure of Salvation' was a much more intense and sobering experience."

Opposite: Baltar faces brutal torture at the hands of the Cylons in 'A Measure of Salvation'.

Above: After the writing staff toyed with the idea of making Sharon Agathon prevent the annihilation of the Cylons, Sharon's actions were shifted to her human husband, Karl 'Helo' Agathon.

By the time Angeli joined *Battlestar Galactica* as a co-executive producer on its third season, the writing staff had already penned a one-page story outline for 'A Measure of Salvation'. This outline provided a broad basis for the episode and explained how it would conclude the Cylon virus plotline established in 'Torn'.

"Some of the elements were in the original outline, but the episode changed a bit when it went to script," Angeli explains. "As I recall, the episode was slightly more of an action-orientated type show in the beginning. But as we got into the script, it became even more of a debate about whether the *Galactica* crew could be accused of genocide if they destroyed these machines who are intent on destroying them."

"That debate raised a lot of questions in the writers' room," continues Anne Cofell Saunders, who scripted 'Torn' and worked with the writing staff on the original outline for 'A Measure of Salvation'. "We found ourselves asking questions like, how would the threat of Cylon genocide affect Sharon and Helo? How could it divide the crew? What would Adama and Laura ultimately decide to do? For about five seconds in the writers' room we even explored what would happen if the humans did release the virus. A lot of the scenes in the episode reflect the discussions we had in the writers' room."

Early versions of the storyline for 'A Measure of Salvation' climaxed with Sharon Agathon thwarting Roslin's plan by executing the Cylon prisoners. Sharon's actions were shifted to Helo by Ronald D. Moore, who felt that Sharon would not betray the oath she had recently taken to her commanders — even at the expense of her own race's existence.

"We really punched up Helo's role as the story developed," Angeli recalls. "The *Galactica*'s plan was also simplified. In early versions of the script, the *Galactica* crew also dropped the beacon into space and Baltar was somehow going to sense that the *Galactica* crew were setting a trap and tell the Cylons to Jump away, in an effort to save his own skin."

Helo's increased role in 'A Measure of Salvation' was appreciated by Karl Agathon's real-life counterpart, Tahmoh Penikett. "I was surprised by what Helo does in that episode, but I was game for it," Penikett reveals. "I found it totally believable that he was willing to go that far, to do what he thinks is the right thing.

SURVEILLANCE: ADDITIONAL

Much of Lee Adama's involvement in 'A Measure of Salvation' was shaped by the producers' early plans for the character's development in season three. "Lee's participation in the trip to the infected Cylon Basestar was originally scripted as part of his evolution into a hard-line marine officer," Ronald D. Moore reveals. "You can also see that in the way he comes up with the idea of using the virus to annihilate the Cylons."

"The one single thing I didn't quite agree with on that episode was the line where Helo says that the Cylons tried to live with us on New Caprica," he reveals. "I don't think he meant that, but I had to play it. So I tried to play it in a way that suggested he was so desperate to make his case, he said that without thinking."

The B-plot of 'A Measure of Salvation' sees Baltar being interrogated and tortured by the Cylons and developing his bond with D'Anna Biers. Moore suggested this scenario to the writing staff, after James Callis casually asked him what would happen if the Cylons started torturing Baltar aboard the Basestar. Unsurprisingly, the intense torture sequences — and their combination with sexual imagery — proved contentious with the US Sci Fi Channel.

"There was a lot more sex in the torture sequences originally," Moore reveals. "We had to tone a lot of things down, but that was okay — we understood where the network was coming from and the idea behind the sequences is still there."

'A Measure of Salvation' was brought to the screen by first-time *Battlestar Galactica* director Bill Eagles, who had previously helmed episodes of such shows as *CSI: Crime Scene Investigation* and *Numb3rs*, plus the 2006 BBC TV movie *Dracula*.

Following principal photography, scenes dropped from the episode for timing reasons included Admiral Adama surveying the infected Cylon Basestar from a Raptor piloted by Sharon Agathon, and Kara Thrace's interrogation of a dying Leoben imprisoned on the *Galactica*.

"I loved that scene," says Callum Keith Rennie of his character's psychological battle with Kara in the episode. "I really liked the way it was reminiscent of season one's 'Flesh and Bone'. It was great. I was surprised we didn't see it in the final cut."

"I liked the scene, but it felt tangential to the episode," Moore explains. "It didn't say anything new or really go anywhere."

Another scene scripted for 'A Measure of Salvation' was dropped at the suggestion of Michael Hogan. It involved Tigh challenging Helo's work as the *Galactica*'s Executive Officer and his marriage to a Cylon. "It was an interesting scene, but I didn't think it made sense in the context of the previous episode," Hogan explains. "At the end of 'Torn', Tigh tells Adama he's not the man he was and he wouldn't see him again. So when I saw they had me in this scene with Helo in the next episode, I immediately called David Eick and told him I felt we needed to lose it. Eick was really upset to hear that, because it was a scene that everyone loved. But they agreed to take me out of that episode, which really shows how the people making this series listen to the actors."

While the show's producers were saddened by the loss of Tigh's single scene in 'A Measure of Salvation', they do not believe it did any harm to the finished product. "I think the episode succeeds as a dramatic examination of moral issues that are relevant to what's happening today on our own planet," Angeli declares. "I found it interesting and provocative, and it's also beautifully played by our cast." ∎

[HERO]

WRITER: David Eick
DIRECTOR: Michael Rymer

GUEST CAST: Carl Lumbly (Lieutenant Daniel 'Bulldog' Novacek), Lucy Lawless (D'Anna Biers), Matthew Bennett (Aaron Doral), Tiffany Lyndall-Knight (The Hybrid), Luciana Carro (Captain Louanne 'Kat' Katraine), Barry Kennedy (Admiral Corman)

> *"I started it. I initiated it... The attacks on the Colonies. By crossing the Line, I showed them we were the warmongers they figured us to be."*
> — Admiral William Adama

On the eve of the forty-fifth anniversary of Admiral Adama's recruitment into the Colonial fleet, the *Galactica* detects a Cylon Raider under Cylon attack. Adama is stunned to discover the Raider is carrying an escaped prisoner, Danny 'Bulldog' Novacek — a former member of his crew aboard the Battlestar *Valkyrie*.

Bulldog tells Adama he has spent the last three years as a prisoner of the Cylons, after he was shot down and captured while on a reconnaissance mission into Cylon space. What Novacek doesn't know, however, is that he was actually shot down by the *Valkyrie*, on Adama's orders, in an effort to conceal the Colonials' excursion into Cylon space.

After Novacek learns the truth from Tigh, he angrily confronts the Admiral. Wracked with guilt over the realization that the black ops mission could have provoked the Cylons into mounting their attack on the Colonies, Adama puts up no resistance to Novacek's attack. But Tigh rushes to Adama's aid and tells Novacek that Kara Thrace has discovered evidence that the Cylons let him go in the hope he would kill Adama.

As Novacek embarks on a new life away from the *Galactica*, Adama offers President Roslin his resignation. Instead, however, she insists he takes a different penance — publicly receive the Medal of Distinction and continue to be regarded as a hero by his crew.

SURVEILLANCE: ADDITIONAL

Novacek's capture by the Cylons was loosely inspired by a real-life military incident — the Soviet Union's capture of a U2 spy plane piloted by CIA agent Francis Gary Powers in 1960.

After scripting the story arc-heavy episodes 'Home, Part I' and 'Home, Part II' in season two, David Eick was happy to write the first stand-alone story of *Battlestar Galactica*'s third season. He also welcomed the opportunity to develop a powerful and provocative character-based drama that firmly focused on William Adama. "Part of the fun of working on *Battlestar Galactica* has always been dealing with the humanity of our characters," Eick explains. "Our protagonists are heroes, but we don't shy away from their faults and failings — we show their feet of clay but then ask viewers to love them anyway.

"Essentially, 'Hero' is all about Adama's interpretation of events leading up to the Cylon attack and the guilt he feels. We never wanted to actually say that Adama was directly responsible for the attack on the Colonies; we simply wanted to explore the idea that he did — for right or wrong — feel some degree of responsibility about it. The

episode is called 'Hero' because Adama's penance at the end of the episode is to carry on as the heroic leader and role model people see him as, despite his own personal feelings."

Eick's storyline for 'Hero' was developed from an idea David Weddle and Bradley Thompson had originally suggested during *Battlestar Galactica*'s second season. "We proposed a story in which a present dilemma causes Adama to remember an incident before the Cylon attack where he violated the armistice, ran a black op in Cylon space and was forced to leave people behind," Weddle reveals. "Adama is left to wonder if he inadvertently triggered the Cylon attack and confesses this to Lee.

"The idea of Bulldog escaping and returning to tell his tale and the crisis this provokes was something the writing staff, and David Eick in particular, fleshed out. It was an inspired choice because it transformed the story from a reflective piece to a story with immediate urgency and dire consequences, both for the fleet and Adama personally."

Early versions of Eick's storyline for 'Hero' involved Roslin sensing that Adama was hiding something about Bulldog's capture by the Cylons and saw her enlisting Lee Adama to investigate. Lee would then have confronted his father with the truth, in an angry scene that at one point culminated in Adama hitting his son for the first time. The storyline concluded with Adama resigning and turning command of the fleet over to Lee, until the Admiral learned of the Cylon plot and was convinced to stay in command.

"During the making of this episode, we realized that Lee's investigation wasn't as interesting as what the characters — particularly Adama and Tigh — were going through," Ron Moore says of the episode's development. "What really came to the fore was that it was going to be about the return of Tigh. It was the episode that rehabilitated Tigh [through his rescue of Adama at the end] and set up his return to the CIC."

Above: The idea of William Adama participating in a covert mission prior to the Cylon attack on the Colonies was initially discussed during *Battlestar Galactica*'s second season.

"The events in 'Hero' pull Tigh out of his pit," Michael Hogan agrees. "Bulldog's return forces him to get up and deal with a new problem. That seems to be the pattern for Tigh — he's living against his will. He has his duty and knows he has to do it."

'Hero' establishes that William Adama was serving aboard the Battlestar *Valkyrie* just prior to events at the start of the *Battlestar Galactica* miniseries. Although some fans complained this revelation was a violation of the show's continuity, Eick is quick to face this criticism.

"When you watch the miniseries there is this natural assumption that the old commander has been on this ship the whole time — but that's never actually stated anywhere in the series," Eick points out. "We actually did check it, and there was nothing in the show's continuity that makes events in 'Hero' inconsistent. We also all really liked the idea that Adama had been assigned to the *Galactica* as a punishment, which is why we did it."

As the script for 'Hero' took shape, the show's makers began to discuss famous actors who could play Adama's former crewmate, Danny 'Bulldog' Novacek (who at various points in the script's development was named Seamus and then Eugene Novacek). *24* and *The Unit* star Dennis Haysbert was initially considered for the role by director Michael Rymer, along with an actor whom Eick had long wanted to feature in the series: *Cagney & Lacey* and *Alias* alumnus Carl Lumbly.

"I had known Carl from the first pilot I produced, which was *M.A.N.T.I.S.* in 1993," Eick explains. "I had tried to get him on *Battlestar* before, but we couldn't make it work because he was too busy working on other stuff. I was so pleased we got him to play Bulldog, because he was great for that role. He's someone who works well in the gray zone — the way he plays him, you don't know if Novacek is a friend or foe."

"I thought Carl Lumbly was wonderful," Rymer agrees. "Carl made Bulldog feel like a real person. I think the viewer's natural inclination is to distrust the character and not think he is what he seems, but the way Carl plays him you start to trust he is for real. He also did a great job with portraying the twist — that Bulldog had deluded himself into believing he had escaped, but he had actually been released."

The production draft script of the episode concluded with Adama publicly handing his medal to "a true hero" — Saul Tigh — and announcing his reappointment as the *Galactica*'s Executive Officer. Eick dropped this idea at Moore's suggestion. "We went back and forth on that a little bit, but it was probably the right call," Eick notes. "It felt a little too pat and sweet for us that Adama was going to publicly bestow this medal on Tigh. It wrapped everything up a bit too nicely with a ribbon.

"What we have now is a scene I probably spent the least time writing, and yet it's one of the most

SURVEILLANCE: ADDITIONAL

'Hero' advances D'Anna Biers' story arc by establishing she is repeatedly killing herself, in the hope she will see the final five Cylons while downloading into a new body. This element of the story arc was suggested by Michael Angeli early in season three's development, while he was recovering from surgery. "As I was convalescing, I was naturally thinking a lot about death and suddenly hit on this idea that D'Anna would constantly kill herself to try to get this vision," Angeli reveals. "So I shot off this email about it to Ron and he totally went for it."

powerful moments of the episode," Eick continues with a chuckle. "Tigh's final conversation with Adama is much more powerful and much more appropriate to the tone of our show and there's a wonderful bittersweet quality to it."

While Eick and Moore agreed on the need to revise the ending of 'Hero', Eick did not share Moore's objections to the episode's suggestion that the Colonial military might have set Adama up. After heated discussion between the two executive producers, one of the episode's two references to the Admiralty's possible desire to provoke a war made the final cut. Moore and Eick also debated the latest instalment of the Cylon Basestar story arc, which established that Baltar had begun sleeping with D'Anna Biers.

"I thought it was perfectly acceptable to jump forward and just say that after events in 'A Measure of Salvation', Baltar had started an affair with D'Anna," Moore explains. "But I had to argue with various people, including David, to get that on screen."

Ultimately, the makers of *Battlestar Galactica* all feel that 'Hero' succeeded as a worthwhile stand-alone character piece. "I was very happy with the episode," states Eick. "I think it suffered from being squashed into a forty-minute timeslot; we could have used more time to explore Adama's guilt and his relationship with Novacek. All of that was in the script. But I was happy with how Michael Rymer pulled off the eerie, subtle, Hitchcockian anticipation of what Bulldog might do."

"I'm very fond of that episode," Rymer agrees. "Its limitation is that its premise is a bit of a stretch. You have to go with the idea that the Cylons have arranged this complicated conspiracy just to mindfuck with Adama. But if you can go with that, it's a fine character piece that Eddie Olmos and Michael Hogan are wonderful in." ■

[UNFINISHED BUSINESS]

WRITER: Michael Taylor
DIRECTOR: Robert Young

GUEST CAST: Kate Vernon (Ellen Tigh), Luciana Carro (Captain Louanne 'Kat' Katraine), Christian Tessier (Tucker 'Duck' Clellan), Dominic Zamprogna (James 'Jammer' Lyman), Don Thompson (Anthony Figurski), Bodie Olmos (Brendan 'Hotdog' Costanza)

(Shouting) "I love Kara Thrace, and I don't care who frakking knows!"
— Lee Adama

(Shouting) "Kara Thrace loves Lee Adama!" — Kara Thrace

In an attempt to resolve the divisions that have emerged on the *Galactica*, Admiral Adama allows the crew to hold an impromptu boxing tournament where rank is forgotten and crewmembers can challenge any of their colleagues to a fight. As the boxing matches take place, several crewmembers take the opportunity to pursue and resolve grudges from the recent past — especially the time of the Colonial settlement on New Caprica.

Disappointed by Chief Tyrol's earlier decision to leave the *Galactica* to pursue a life on New Caprica, Admiral Adama challenges the Chief to a bloody boxing match. But this bout proves to be just the prelude to the main event: a brutal fight between Lee Adama and Kara Thrace.

Still angered by how Kara spent a passionate night with him on New Caprica, only to marry Samuel Anders the following morning, Lee becomes locked in a bitter battle with his former love. As their fight unfolds, however, Lee and Kara's anger gradually gives way to a revived friendship — and passion — between the two Viper pilots.

Edward James Olmos has no hesitation in naming 'Unfinished Business' as one of the highlights of *Battlestar Galactica*'s third season. "I thought that episode was just unprecedented," he says. "I thought the way Robert Young directed it was quite stellar. It's just psychologically incredible."

Olmos' opinion of 'Unfinished Business' is shared by the majority of his cast and crewmates, including Ronald D. Moore. "It's one of my favourite episodes of the entire series," Moore reveals. "It's really moving and powerful and has some great character moments. It's also a unique episode, in the way it fits into the history of the series."

A loose sequel to the second season finale, 'Lay Down Your Burdens, Part II', 'Unfinished Business' was designed to be the episode that answered viewers' questions about the events that took place on New Caprica between the planet's colonization and the arrival of the Cylons. The episode marked the *Battlestar Galactica* writing début

of Michael Taylor, who found himself scripting 'Unfinished Business' after suggesting an episode could revolve around a boxing match.

Above: Kara Thrace and Samuel Anders after their spontaneous wedding on New Caprica.

"That was my first pitch to the show," Taylor recalls. "I just threw it out — I said, 'There's so much tension on the ship, maybe the crew would want to work it off in a *Fight Club* kind of way.' I was surprised when Ron said, 'Yeah, I like that. We'll do that and throw in the flashbacks!' I then wrote a story document that summarized the present-day storyline and suggested a not terribly well defined past storyline. Ron had a lot of great ideas which I incorporated into the script, and I also got some great notes from Mark Verheiden."

Unusually, scheduling issues meant that the flashback scenes had to be finalized long before the rest of the episode. "The New Caprica scenes had to be shot at the same time as we were doing the first four episodes, as the sets were going to be struck after that," Taylor explains. "After the flashbacks had been shot, I then had to figure out the present-day scenes. It was an interesting challenge to work like that."

The episode's biggest revelation concerns Lee and Kara's passionate fling immediately before Kara's sudden wedding to Sam Anders. This storyline answered the question of what had caused the rift between Lee and Kara.

"It was always my conviction that Lee and Kara had had an affair," Taylor reveals. "The interesting thing for me was trying to work out why these characters did what they did, especially Kara. Kara is such a compelling character — she's screwed up in some ways, yet confident in others — so trying to understand her and her motives really directed what happened in the past."

Taylor and Moore's take on Lee and Kara's tragic fling intrigued both of the characters' real-life counterparts, Jamie Bamber and Katee Sackhoff. "I thought the writers' explanation of the rift was really smart," says Sackhoff. "When I first read the flashback scene to their affair, I cried. I was shocked by it, but it's totally believable. It shows how much Kara loves Lee, and at the same time is terrified of that."

"It was surprising to find out the missing piece of the jigsaw," Bamber agrees. "Yet it was very truthful about the Kara/Lee relationship."

On a far lighter note, 'Unfinished Business' also shows William Adama and Laura Roslin enjoying their most intimate moment together on New Caprica, as they share what the script openly refers to as a joint. "That scene came from what I think was a throwaway note from Ron," Taylor reveals. "When he read my first pass at the flashback scenes he said, 'You could do something in this scene. I don't care if they're getting high, smoking or anything…' Now I don't know if he was joking, but I just went, 'That's a good idea' and I wrote them getting high!"

Taylor's daring "getting high" scene won the approval of not only Moore but also the show's two stars, Edward James Olmos and Mary McDonnell. "I loved it," says McDonnell. "Eddie and I both felt it was an interesting choice, and we knew if we handled it well and Bob handled it well as the director — which he clearly did — it would have resonance, but it wouldn't undermine our ability to trust these characters. It was so delightful to see the sensuality of being on the ground together, out of the ship. I enjoyed the fact that Laura appreciates the sensuality of being on the planet and for a very brief moment in time begins to imagine she could live that way.

"Personally, I didn't have any reservations about that scene — none whatsoever," she says emphatically. "I'm a baby boomer and I was always sort of disappointed at Bill Clinton's 'I didn't inhale' comment. I was very impressed with Barack Obama saying he did!"

Despite the cast and crew's enthusiasm for it, the 'getting high' scene was toned down at the request of the Sci Fi Channel, who had serious concerns about its depiction of Adama and Roslin. "Probably the biggest discussion we had on season three was whether Adama and Roslin smoking a marijuana-like substance was appropriate," confirms Sci Fi Channel executive Mark Stern. "Ron was very strongly in favour of the idea. He didn't think

SURVEILLANCE: ADDITIONAL

Scenes cut from the final version of 'Unfinished Business' included Lee's proposal to Dualla immediately after Kara's marriage to Anders. A brief scene that explained the shift in Kara's relationship with Saul Tigh was also dropped for timing reasons. "It was a little moment that changed the dynamic between the two characters," Moore says of the latter sequence. "Basically, Kara walked back to the encampment after sleeping with Lee and found the only person who was still awake was Tigh — he was still drinking, which is how he keeps hangovers at bay. Tigh offered Kara a drink and then she confessed what was going on, and Tigh just laughed at how screwed up the situation was. Kara also saw the absurdity of the situation and they started laughing together and bonded over that."

Other moments dropped from the finished episode included Admiral Adama bursting into song while relaxing on New Caprica with Laura Roslin. "Eddie sung and made up his own melody," Michael Taylor reveals. "It was a nice scene."

Adama or Roslin were prudish or moralistic. We agreed with that, but we had qualms about showing the two leaders of that society smoking pot. They responded to that by making it ambiguous what exactly they were smoking."

"The network wanted it understated — like they're smoking cigars or something," Taylor confirms. "But the whole idea remains that they're getting totally stoned out of their minds."

Far less controversially, the episode's present-day sequences required several of *Battlestar Galactica*'s leading characters to enter the boxing ring. The contenders include Chief Tyrol, who finds himself reluctantly slugging it out with Admiral Adama in scenes co-ordinated by Aleks Paunovic.

"I was thrilled when I read that script and saw I was gonna kick Adama's ass," Aaron Douglas recalls with a laugh. "Though the boxing was really difficult for me to shoot, because I'd injured myself playing hockey a few weeks earlier. But we got round that by saying the Chief was one of those guys who doesn't move too much — he just stands in the middle of the ring and makes three shots to land one.

"In the end, we had a lot of fun doing that stuff. The great thing about Eddie is that you never know what he's going to do. I actually took several shots from him for real, and I think I laced him with a few too! But he loves it — if you tag him he wants to hit you back. He wanted Adama to be beaten to a pulp; he kept saying, 'More blood!'"

Above: 'Unfinished Business' was designed to address the unanswered questions from the New Caprica story arc — including what caused the breakdown of Lee and Kara's relationship just prior to the Cylons' arrival at the planet.

Karl Agathon similarly got to spar with Lee Adama, after boxing and martial arts enthusiast Tahmoh Penikett asked the show's producers if his character could feature in a fight scene. Penikett's request led to Helo replacing a guest character whom Lee would have quickly knocked-out.

One actor who was glad not to be involved in any of the episode's fight scenes, however, was Alessandro Juliani. "Initially they were going to have Gaeta — in a state of self-loathing — being beaten up by Sharon," he reveals. "I was glad that didn't happen because it seemed a bit weird, on many fronts."

Moore is full of praise for the way the episode's boxing sequences were realised by returning *Battlestar Galactica* director Robert Young. "When I walked on to that set, I felt that I'd actually walked into a boxing match," he recalls. "It just felt so authentic. Everyone was really into it!" ■

[THE PASSAGE]

WRITER: Jane Espenson
DIRECTOR: Michael Nankin

GUEST CAST: Luciana Carro (Captain Louanne 'Kat' Katraine), Lucy Lawless (D'Anna Biers), Leah Cairns (Lieutenant Margaret 'Racetrack' Edmondson), Tiffany Lyndall-Knight (The Hybrid), G. Patrick Currie (Enzo), Bodie Olmos (Lieutenant Brenden 'Hotdog' Costanza), Brad Dryborough (Hoshi), Sebastian Spence (Lieutenant Noel 'Narcho' Allison)

> "When you were CAG you protected your people, made them feel safe enough to be brave. What you were going to say, does it change that?"
> — Admiral Adama, to Captain Louanne 'Kat' Katraine

After the fleet's food supplies are contaminated, humankind's only hope of survival lies on a planet rich in edible algae. But reaching the planet will require a journey through a massive star cluster that will disable the navigation systems of the civilian ships and expose their occupants to potentially lethal levels of radiation.

With the food shortage mounting, Admiral Adama develops a plan to take civilians through the star cluster on the radiation-shielded *Galactica* and use the Battlestar's Raptors to guide the civilian ships through the cluster. Each trip is grueling for the Raptor pilots, who must carefully monitor how much radiation they are exposed to.

Above: Kara Thrace and the rest of the *Galactica*'s Viper pilots face one of their most dangerous assignments yet in 'The Passage'.

As civilians board the *Galactica*, Louanne 'Kat' Katraine encounters a former lover — Enzo. Enzo reminds Kat of her dark past as a drug runner. Haunted by guilt and Kara Thrace's discovery of her true identity, Kat heroically gives her life completing a fatal fifth and final run through the star cluster.

Meanwhile, Gaius Baltar discovers that D'Anna has been using the power of downloading in her search for answers. He tells her he shares her desire to know who the final five Cylons are, as he hopes he is one of them. Following a cryptic discussion with The Cylon Hybrid, Baltar suggests that D'Anna may find her answers on a planet situated near a star cluster…

SURVEILLANCE: ADDITIONAL

Various subplots and scenes were developed and abandoned during the making of 'The Passage'. These included Helo's fear at being exposed to radiation following his months on Caprica, the availability of radiation medication that was being reserved for Admiral Adama and President Roslin, and a sequence in which Helo and Sharon discussed the loss of Hera. A light-hearted scene in which Kara and Lee are seemingly chewing gum, only for it to be revealed that they are chewing paper, was also left on the cutting room floor.

A B-plot involving Laura starting to experience shared visions with Sharon Agathon was also cut from this episode. This long-planned development was reworked for the season finale, 'Crossroads'.

'The Passage' enabled Ronald D. Moore to pursue two story concepts he had long been keen to explore. "We had kicked around the idea of doing an episode involving a food shortage for quite a while," Moore explains. "I had also

wanted to do an episode where the *Galactica* had to run a gauntlet, like a naval ship passing through a storm. I thought those two ideas were true to the reality of the characters' situation and their quest for survival alone in the universe."

The episode's premise was initially developed by the series' writing staff, who enlisted the advice of *Battlestar Galactica*'s science consultant, Dr Kevin Grazier, to decide on the space phenomenon the fleet would have to navigate. After discussing numerous options (including the possibility of the algae planet actually being located inside the star cluster), the writers settled on the idea that the *Galactica*'s voyage to the planet would simply be blocked by the star cluster. Moore also determined that the crew's main threat would be a visceral, real-world danger: radiation.

To give events in 'The Passage' added impact and meaning, Moore announced that a familiar character would have to die as a result of radiation exposure. The writing staff quickly settled on the idea of giving Louanne Katraine a heroic send-off.

"As much as we loved the character, we all really sparked to the idea that this would be Kat's send-off," Moore reveals. "Kat was someone we had watched become a pilot and a trusted and loved member of the crew, so we knew her death would be a real loss."

With the episode's storyline in place, Moore decided to assign scripting duties to Jane Espenson. A veteran writer/producer whose credits include *Buffy the Vampire Slayer*, *Angel*, *Firefly*, *The OC* and *Star Trek: Deep Space Nine* (the show which marked her first collaboration with Moore), Espenson had recently asked *Battlestar Galactica*'s producers about the possibility of writing for their show.

"I met with Ron Moore and David Eick and, quite honestly, I just flat out begged 'em!" Espenson recalls with a laugh. "I already loved the show. The world, the characters... everything feels so real and complete. The idea of playing in that sandbox was just fantastic. I was thrilled when they called me back in and handed me an episode to write."

While the basic structure of the episode was in place by the time of Espenson's hiring, the writer was encouraged to change and develop the storyline in any ways she felt fit. One of her key contributions concerned the nature of Kat's dark past.

"The original concept was that Kat had been a drug-runner," Espenson reveals, "but Ron then suggested that we needed something bigger. So I came up with the notion that she'd smuggled people and the idea that could be tied to the Cylon attack. The original storyline also had three or four people from Kat's past showing up among the Thera Sita passengers. I pared that back to one ex-boyfriend, which was much easier to handle."

Another Espenson addition to the episode allowed the writer to bring her trademark comedy to *Battlestar Galactica*. "I love the paper shortage/hysterical laughter scene with Adama and Tigh," she says with a smile. "I wanted some really dark

---

SURVEILLANCE: ADDITIONAL ||||▶

Following production on 'The Passage', an additional scene featuring Captain Katraine and Admiral Adama was written and shot for the expanded, two-part version of 'Exodus'. Set directly before the New Caprica rescue mission, the scene saw Adama telling Kat he trusted her and was designed to emphasize her importance to the crew. Ironically, the scene ultimately didn't make the final cut of the episode.

humor to emerge from the starvation and I was so pleased that moment survived into the finished episode."

Espenson's script was assigned to director Michael Nankin, who had previously helmed the pivotal Kat episode 'Scar'. Unfortunately, by the time the script was distributed to the series' cast and crew, neither Moore nor David Eick had managed to warn Luciana Carro about her character's demise. "I had no idea that was coming," Carro confirms. "I only found out about Kat's death from my roommate!

"I was flying from Los Angeles to Vancouver to shoot 'Unfinished Business' when my roommate called me to say she'd got the script for 'The Passage' and that it was centred around my character. She was so excited about my role and all the information that was coming out about Kat's background. When I heard about that I said, 'Can you do me a favour? Can you check the last page and see what it says?' And she said, 'Oh no… They've put Kat's picture on the Memorial Wall!' I was like 'What?!' I couldn't believe it. So I was there in the airport, crying. It wasn't the ideal way to find out, but these things happen."

Above: Kat's dying exchange with Admiral Adama was a highlight of the episode for Luciana Carro.

"I do still feel bad about the way Luciana found out," Moore admits. "It was every producer's nightmare come true!"

Fortunately, once the initial shock of her character's demise had passed, Carro was thrilled by the way 'The Passage' allowed her character to bow out of the series. "I thought the episode was great," she states. "It gives Kat a very heroic send-off and it really explains a lot of things about her — why she had issues with authority and why she was always trying to prove herself. Kat always wanted to prove that she was a good person, and she does it in that episode. I thought that was great.

"Obviously, I would have preferred not to have been killed off," she notes. "I do feel there was a lot more they could have done with Kat. But I completely understand why they did it and my death scene was really great. I'd always wanted to do a scene like that with Eddie, where Adama is like Kat's father. That was actually the last scene I shot and it was very emotional.

"I was surprised by just how strongly the crew was affected by Kat's death," she adds. "When we were shooting the episode, several crewmembers tried to rewrite the ending to keep Kat's fate open. They suggested she was a Cylon, or a spirit guide, or something. They would give me these new pages of the script and I would be like, 'Don't give them to me, give them to Ron!'" she laughs.

As painful as it was for the cast and crew, Kat's heroic demise helped make 'The Passage' a strong instalment of season three. "I like 'The Passage' a lot," says Moore. "It's one of the most harrowing episodes we've done and I think the revelations about Kat are really interesting." ■

[THE EYE OF JUPITER]

WRITER: Mark Verheiden
DIRECTOR: Michael Rymer

GUEST CAST: Lucy Lawless (D'Anna Biers), Dean Stockwell (Brother Cavil), Callum Keith Rennie (Leoben Conoy), Tiffany Lyndall-Knight (The Hybrid), Eileen Pedde (Gunnery Sergeant Erin Mathias), Brad Dryborough (Lieutenant Hoshi), Alisen Down (Jean Barolay), Aleks Paunovic (Marine Sergeant Omar Fischer), Diego Diablo Del Mar (Hillard)

"Make any attempt to attack this ship or the people on the planet surface, I'll launch every nuke I've got... lay waste to the entire continent."
— Admiral William Adama, to D'Anna Biers

Two weeks into the algae collection mission, Chief Tyrol finds himself mysteriously drawn to the location of the Temple of Five — the fabled home of the Eye of Jupiter, which is said to guide those who discover it to Earth. As Tyrol searches for the Eye of Jupiter, four Cylon Basestars Jump into the vicinity of the algae planet.

A Cylon party including Gaius Baltar meet with Admiral Adama and President Roslin aboard the *Galactica*. The Cylons make Adama and Roslin an offer: in return for the Eye of Jupiter, they will allow the people on the algae planet to leave unharmed. Adama responds by warning the Cylons that if they attempt to find the Eye of Jupiter, he will unleash a nuclear strike on the planet. Adama later tells the ground crew they must destroy the Temple if the Cylons reach it.

Aboard one of the Cylon Basestars, D'Anna reveals that she secretly dispatched a Cylon Heavy Raider to the algae planet on the Cylons' arrival in the system. Lee Adama reluctantly enlists Sam Anders' help in organizing a defence plan against the Cylon Centurions — but the pair violently clash after Kara Thrace's Raptor is shot down by the Cylons.

Obsessed by her desire to see the faces of the final five Cylons, D'Anna and Baltar decide they must visit the planet surface. As six Cylon Heavy Raiders head to the planet, Adama prepares to launch a nuclear strike...

'The Eye of Jupiter' and 'Rapture' were designed to be the episodes which ended season three's Cylon Basestar story arc and enabled Baltar's return to the *Galactica*. The episodes' main plotline was partly inspired by a suggestion from David Weddle and Bradley Thompson.

"'The Eye of Jupiter' and 'Rapture' originally grew out of a desire that Brad and I had for the humans and Cylons to fight over a piece of real estate," Weddle explains.

Opposite: Chief Tyrol finds himself mysteriously drawn to the Temple of Five in 'The Eye of Jupiter'.

"The World War II analogy this time was the battle for Guadalcanal, which my father took part in as a US marine. We thought something analogous to that would provide a good venue for doing a ground combat episode between humans and Cylons. We wanted to dramatize how common infantry soldiers are often asked to perform almost impossible tasks — to take a hill or to hold one, to dig in or move out, or fall back — often without knowing why, or for reasons that seem insane or absurd to them.

"The trick was to figure out the strategic object that the humans and Cylons would fight over. In the mythos it seemed to make the most sense that they would find another remnant left behind by the Thirteenth Tribe of Man that would provide a clue about the path to Earth."

While Weddle and Thompson wrote the second part of the storyline, Mark Verheiden scripted the opener. "Knowing that 'The Eye of Jupiter' would be the last episode before the mid-season break [on the US Sci Fi Channel], we definitely wanted it to rev up the Earth storyline and leave some things hanging so folks would come back for the next round," Verheiden says of the assignment. "We also knew that we wanted to wrap up the Cylon/Baltar storyline and move on to other topics. One of the challenges presented by the episodes was pulling together a lot of hanging plot threads and preparing to forge ahead in a new direction."

"Part of the rationale of doing this two-parter was servicing the larger storyline of the show," adds Ronald D. Moore. "We had done a lot of personal episodes and an action space show, so it was time to return to the mythology and the search for Earth."

Another vital element of the two-parter was provided by the "love quadrangle" between Lee, Kara, Anders and Dualla, which had developed as a result of events in 'Unfinished Business'. "I thought Lee and Kara having an affair was very interesting," Moore explains. "I really liked the idea that they would become trapped, because Kara won't divorce Anders and Lee won't cheat on Dualla."

The core storyline of 'The Eye of Jupiter' and 'Rapture' changed very little during the development and shooting of the episodes, with only various elements of the plot undergoing minor changes. While early versions of 'The Eye of Jupiter' saw Tyrol and Cally discovering an ancient city that had become buried over many years, and ultimately discovering the Temple of Five by accidentally falling through its roof, this idea was simplified to what Moore refers to as "a *Close Encounters* moment" for budgetary reasons. Various ways of Sharon Agathon discovering the truth about Hera were also briefly considered, including the Boomer Sharon giving her a chip that mentally projected Athena to the Cylon Basestar. A sequence in which Baltar secretly gave Gaeta valuable information about the instability of the system's star while

SURVEILLANCE: ADDITIONAL

'The Eye of Jupiter' was initially titled 'The Eye of Zeus'. "We changed the name simply because 'The Eye of Zeus' somehow seemed a bit too mystical and over the top, even for us," explains Ronald D. Moore. "'The Eye of Jupiter' somehow sounded a little less hokey. It was also a nice way to broaden the pantheon of the gods in the *Galactica* universe and the mythos, as Zeus was the Greek name for the father of the gods and Jupiter was the later Roman version of that idea."

aboard the *Galactica* was similarly abandoned in favour of Gaeta making the discovery by himself.

On beginning work on the two-parter, director Michael Rymer immediately made it clear that the episodes' exterior shots would require a distinctive look that couldn't be captured at the series' regular filming locations. "It was a line in the sand for me — I stated that if we were going to go to another planet, it couldn't look like Stanley Park; we had to show some other terrain," Rymer explains. "Fortunately, everyone agreed with me. So we settled on the idea of going on location to Kamloops."

A four-hour drive from Vancouver Film Studios, Kamloops had previously been considered as a possible setting for the New Caprica scenes in 'Lay Down Your Burdens, Part II'. An area near East Shuswap Road provided the backdrop for the bulk of the exterior sequences set on the algae planet, while the scenes set in the Raptor and tent were filmed on the show's regular soundstages in Vancouver.

The change of scenery was not only appreciated by *Battlestar Galactica*'s viewers, but was also enjoyed by the series' cast and crew. "That was the first time we'd gone somewhere and had an overnight stay," says Aaron Douglas. "It was fun for all of us to get away from the usual routine and hang out with each other.

"Another thing that was great about going to Kamloops was that my best friend from high school, Jason Lumley, lives there," Douglas continues. "He's a prison guard and he loves the show, so I got him a role as an extra."

As well as propelling the characters into a new environment, 'The Eye of Jupiter' also sees Samuel T. Anders finally confronting Lee Adama about his feelings for Kara. "That was something we had all been waiting for," Michael Trucco notes. "It was great to see Anders confront Lee over his affair with Kara, under the guise of a military operation. It was amazing to work with Jamie Bamber on that, and for us to get in each other's faces. I thought it was a pretty good pissing match!"

"I loved that," Bamber agrees. "I loved the complicated mix of personal conflict in an epic situation and I enjoyed playing it with Michael Trucco. I thought the idea of Lee having to put his wife in the line of fire to save Starbuck, who he feels more for, was just terrific."

The episode's cliffhanger ending was initially set to involve a stand-off between Anders and Lee, with the two leaders and their respective groups all pointing guns at one another. This idea was abandoned at the suggestion of Michael Rymer, who felt it was melodramatic and unconvincing. The Lee/Anders confrontation was replaced by a different stand-off which had initially taken place earlier, in the episode's third act.

"The stand-off between Adama and the Cylons became the cliffhanger because it felt like a really strong ending," Moore explains. "It's reminiscent of the stand-off scenes in good submarine movies like *The Hunt for Red October* and *Crimson Tide*. There's a lot of jeopardy and unanswered questions at the end of the episode." ■

SURVEILLANCE: ADDITIONAL

Leoben's repeated observation that "All this has happened before and it will all happen again" was actually inspired by the narration of the 1953 animated Disney film *Peter Pan*.

[RAPTURE]

WRITERS: David Weddle & Bradley Thompson
DIRECTOR: Michael Rymer

GUEST CAST: Lucy Lawless (D'Anna Biers), Dean Stockwell (Brother Cavil), Callum Keith Rennie (Leoben Conoy), Eileen Pedde (Gunnery Sergeant Erin Mathias), Alisen Down (Jean Barolay), Lily Duong-Walton (Hera Agathon), Diego Diablo Del Mar (Hillard), Brad Dryborough (Hoshi), Aleks Paunovic (Marine Sergeant Omar Fischer), Tygh Runyan (Private Sykes)

"There are five other Cylons, Brother. I saw them. One day you're going to see them too..." — D'Anna Biers, to Brother Cavil

---

Faced with the threat of a nuclear strike on the planet, the Cylons agree that their Heavy Raiders should return to the Basestar. But the ship containing D'Anna and Baltar continues to the planet — much to the disgust of her fellow Cylons. Admiral Adama decides to allow the ship to land rather than launch the attack.

As a team of marines and civilians battle the Cylon forces heading for the Temple of Five, Lee Adama secures Anders' support by ordering Dualla to locate and rescue Kara Thrace. When the defence force is unable to stop D'Anna and Baltar reaching the Temple, Lee Adama orders Tyrol to destroy it — but the Cylons defuse the explosives before he can complete his mission. D'Anna dies after experiencing a vision of the final five Cylons, while Baltar is captured by Tyrol. Following her decision to disobey the wishes of the other Cylons, the D'Anna model of Cylon is permanently boxed.

The ground team returns to the *Galactica* just in time to escape the planet's destruction, as a result of its star going supernova. They are joined on the Battlestar by Hera Agathon — whom Sharon rescues after being shot by Helo and downloading aboard the Cylon Basestar. Sharon's return to the *Galactica* is aided by Caprica Six.

Following their escape, the *Galactica* crew notice that the supernova resembles the mandala inside the Eye of Jupiter — and realize the mandala was meant to lead them to the Ionian nebula...

Karl Agathon's murder of his wife, the 'Athena' Sharon, was originally scripted and filmed as part of the cliffhanger ending to 'The Eye of Jupiter'. This scene — which replaced earlier plans for Sharon to fly a stolen Raptor into the Cylon Basestar — became the teaser to 'Rapture' after the previous episode's cliffhanger had been reworked.

"That was probably my favourite scene of the season," says Grace Park of her character's (temporary) demise. "I felt it was so intense and really moving."

Above: Lee Adama faces the Cylons on the algae planet — in a scene shot on location in Kamloops.

"It was one of the most emotional scenes I've done on the show," Tahmoh Penikett agrees. "I loved doing that scene, and the scene just after that where Helo loses it with the President. That was a huge moment for me."

"I thought Sharon's death was really shocking and emotional," adds Ronald D. Moore. "It was an interesting idea to have her killed by Helo, and it gave us a really good teaser."

Following her death, Athena downloads aboard the Cylon Basestar in an attempt to rescue Hera. Before she completes her mission, the 'Boomer' Sharon threatens to kill Hera in a scene that proved highly controversial with the US Sci Fi Channel. "We had a lot of back and forth on that," Moore recalls. "It took a lot of time to agree what we were going to show."

As the Sharon plotline unfolds, 'Rapture' continues the struggle between the ground crew and the Cylons over the Temple of Five. The ground assault scenes on the algae planet were devised and choreographed by writers David Weddle and Bradley Thompson, who visited Kamloops during location shooting to ensure the sequences' military authenticity. Drawing inspiration from John F. Antal's account of the March 1943 battle of El Guettar in his book *Infantry Combat: The Rifle Platoon*, the pair initially developed an intricate defence plan for Lee Adama to implement — a plan that involved several pieces of tactical manoeuvring, large numbers of troops and the use of Tylium fires.

Unfortunately, a combination of timing and

SURVEILLANCE: ADDITIONAL

The nature of Baltar's return to the *Galactica* was improvised by Michael Rymer and James Callis during the shooting of 'Rapture'. "The first I heard about it was when I got a call from Universal asking me why we'd put Baltar in a body bag," recalls Ronald D. Moore with a grin. "I told them it was a complicated decision and we'd talk about it at our next meeting, and then I called the set and asked them why they'd done that! It was a really smart idea though, because it brought Baltar back to the ship without having to play him in chains or anything else."

budgetary restraints meant that Weddle and Thompson had to rework their vision during production.

"We rewrote the battle with a miniscule Colonial force, one Raptor and one Heavy Raider full of Cylons," Thompson explains. "Personally, I think the intimacy of the small numbers worked to our advantage dramatically. Sometimes it's good not to have all the money you want. But I would have loved to see the Tylium cook the Centurions — Gary Hutzel and the visual effects crew would have made spectacular work of it."

While the ground battle rages, the algae planet also plays host to Dualla's rescue of Kara following her crash-landing in the closing moments of 'The Eye of Jupiter'. An early version of this storyline involved Kara injuring her leg and being carried back to the base by Dualla, but this idea had to be revised to allow her scenes with Dualla to be confined to a soundstage-based Raptor.

"After production analyzed the script, they told us there was no way we had the money for Dualla to drag Kara across a day of locations," Thompson recalls. "If all their conversations could happen in a Raptor, we could shoot it on our sets. So David and I came up with Kara's burned hands as the most effective way to make Starbuck unable to fly. We'd read reports of pilots burning their hands trying to get out of shot-up airplanes and it's a horrible injury. The idea that Kara was a good enough flight instructor to be able to talk Dualla through take-off, orbital entry and a trap — an arrested landing — aboard a Battlestar while in pain and blasted on morpha really appealed to us. It also made both of them instrumental in each other's survival, which worked better for the characters. It was another case of budget forcing us into better drama."

Dualla's rescue of Starbuck proved to be a highlight of season three for Kandyse McClure. "I was very excited about that storyline," she says. "I love Dualla's reaction to Lee asking her to save Starbuck and I was so glad we got to see that Dualla knows what's going on between Kara and Lee. I think that storyline turned out well.

"The other thing that excited me about

SURVEILLANCE: ADDITIONAL

The conclusion of 'Rapture' returns to another aspect of the series' story arc, with Kara recognizing the mandala from the Temple of Five. This scene was prompted by a request from Ronald D. Moore. "Ron said he wanted Kara to see something on the temple that no one else understands — something like a passage of writing that only she, for some metaphysical reason, is able to read and interpret," David Weddle reveals. "He wanted this to play upon Leoben's insistence that Starbuck is special and has a destiny to fulfil. While we were writing the episode we struggled to find the right idea — one that wouldn't be too hokey. We finally remembered the mandala on the wall of Kara's apartment on Caprica, the one she and Helo visited in 'Valley of Darkness'. This seemed perfect to us, so we wrote the final scene where Helo compares the mandala on the temple to the one Kara painted and she realizes Leoben may have been telling her the truth."

'Rapture' was that Dualla got a gun and finally got to show the soldier she is," McClure laughs. "I'd been waiting two and a half years for that."

The closing moments of 'Rapture' see the *Galactica* crew gaining a new clue to the route to Earth. However, the form that clue would take was the subject of lengthy debate in the writers' room.

"At first, we wanted to avoid doing the 'Well of Lost Souls' [from *Raiders of the Lost Ark*], with the sun and light showing the way," Moore explains. "So we discussed various other ideas and then ultimately we said, 'No, it *is* the Well of Lost Souls.' That was the simplest and most effective way of doing it."

The episode's climax was also designed to wrap D'Anna Biers' story arc, with D'Anna reaching the Temple of Five (which in reality was the same disused potash silo within the British Columbia Railyards that had previously doubled as parts of Ragnar Station in the *Battlestar Galactica* miniseries). At the suggestion of

Opposite & Above: Anders and Lee are relieved to see Dualla and Kara managed to escape the algae planet.

Michael Rymer, the culmination of D'Anna's quest also required a return visit to the Vancouver's Orpheum Theatre, which again doubled as the Kobol Opera House first seen in 'Kobol's Last Gleaming'. Surprisingly, at the time D'Anna's vision of the final five was written and shot, the show's makers deliberately left it open — even for themselves — which of the five D'Anna was apologizing to.

"At the time we shot that scene, we had no idea who D'Anna was talking to," Rymer admits. "I know after the season finale aired people started to think it was meant to be Tigh, but my own feeling is that she's talking to the Cylon we have yet to discover. Only time will tell."

D'Anna's vision leads to her entire model of Cylon being 'boxed' as a punishment. This conclusion to D'Anna's story arc was exactly as Moore had planned from the beginning of season three. "We had always talked about bringing Lucy Lawless back for a ten-episode arc and ending it with her being boxed," he states. "Everything in her entire storyline led to this moment."

"The arc of the character was pretty much what we discussed at the beginning," Lawless confirms. "They just filled in some blanks along the way. I thought it was great. I feel that the character was really explored and utilized in a wonderful way, so I'm grateful for the opportunity I got to do it.

"I loved the ending," she continues with a smile. "It's so funny that D'Anna gets shrunk down basically into a cigarette box and put in Cavil's pocket, because Dean Stockwell and I had always played it that Cavil had a thing for D'Anna and wasn't happy she went off with Baltar and Six. But at the end, he gets all of them!" ∎

[TAKING A BREAK FROM ALL YOUR WORRIES]

WRITER: Michael Taylor
DIRECTOR: Edward James Olmos

GUEST CAST: Kerry Norton (Layne Ishay), Leah Cairns (Lieutenant Margaret 'Racetrack' Edmondson), Tom Bower (Joe), Steve Lawlor (Guard), Graeme Duffy (Adrien Bauer), Jason Bryden (Knucklehead Dragger #1)

"I am not a murderer! I am innocent! Why won't you believe me?"
— Gaius Baltar

Sleep deprived and on a hunger strike in his *Galactica* prison cell, Gaius Baltar decides to kill himself, in the hope that — as a Cylon — he will awaken on a Resurrection Ship. But after his suicide attempt is interrupted by Gaeta, Baltar is injected with potent hallucinogens and interrogated by President Roslin and Admiral Adama about his involvement with the Cylons and their knowledge about the whereabouts of Earth. In his drug-induced state, Baltar denies that he ever knowingly conspired with the Cylons and reveals he no longer believes he is a Cylon.

Following his interrogation, Baltar is visited by Gaeta in his cell. Gaeta tries to murder the former President, but Baltar is saved by Adama and Roslin. Roslin then tells Adama that she has decided Baltar will stand trial for his crimes.

Meanwhile, Lee Adama's relationship with Dualla continues to disintegrate. But when Kara tells him she will leave Anders to be with him, Lee dismisses the idea and instead attempts to renew his commitment to his wife…

SURVEILLANCE: ADDITIONAL

The title of 'Taking a Break From All Your Worries' was inspired by the lyrics of the theme song to the Boston bar-based sitcom *Cheers*. "It originally came from the idea that Lee was looking for a respite from his marital woes in this bar," Michael Taylor explains. "For me, the title now has a pleasant ironic texture, given the awful treatment Baltar gets. He is hardly taking a break from his worries!"

As its title suggests, 'Taking a Break From All Your Worries' was initially devised as a much lighter episode than the hard-hitting drama it turned out to be. "It was supposed to be a comedy episode," writer Michael Taylor explains with a laugh. "It was originally going to be about Lee turning a ship into a replacement for Cloud Nine — he was going to open a casino ship or a resort ship. That idea got scaled down to him creating a bar, then him saving a bar. I thought it worked pretty well. It was a funny story.

"But then Jamie Bamber raised some concerns about the episode," he continues. "He thought Lee's whole relationship with Dualla and their problems were getting short changed and being dealt with too lightly. He felt Dualla had to pull Lee up on not being a good husband. I discussed Jamie's thoughts with Ron Moore and Ron said, 'Okay, if that's how Jamie feels, let's try another tack.' So I rewrote half the script and came up with a different story for Lee."

"Lee's original storyline was inspired by the character Milo Minderbinder, the supply guy in *Catch-22*, and the episode of *M*A*S*H* where Hawkeye has to do a long chain of trades to get a fresh pair of boots," Ronald D. Moore adds. "It was a nice

idea and well executed, yet it never quite gelled for me, so we decided to move the episode towards it being more about the problems in Lee and Dualla's marriage."

As Taylor's rewrite took shape and its comedy tone faded, the writer discovered the episode's planned B-plot became increasingly important. "Baltar's storyline started to naturally come to the fore as the episode developed," he recalls. "You could say it was the B-story that became the A-story.

"'Taking a Break' really emerged as our Guantánamo Bay episode. Some of the stuff that was done to Baltar, like sleep deprivation and force feeding, is I believe all being done at Guantánamo Bay. Even the drug torture was something from the annals of the CIA's experimentation with LSD torture."

At one point in the episode's development, Baltar's torture was set to disgust paramedic Layne Ashay to such an extent that she leaked information of his treatment to the press. But this plot did not make the finished episode, due to timing constraints.

One element of the episode that did remain constant, however, was the introduction of the show's new recurring resort location — Joe's Bar (which was initially called 'The Y-Not' in Taylor's script). "When we blew up Cloud Nine at the end of season two, we did so on the explicit understanding that we would eventually establish a new place for the characters to go and relax and enjoy themselves," says Moore. "That was something important to the network and to us internally."

Above: 'Taking a Break From All Your Worries' was originally devised as a light-hearted episode for Lee Adama, but was reworked at the request of Jamie Bamber.

Due to a combination of production and scheduling factors, 'Taking a Break From All Your Worries' was assigned to be directed by *Battlestar Galactica*'s leading man, Edward James Olmos. By nothing more than sheer coincidence, Olmos had previously helmed the series' earlier attempt at a comedy-orientated episode, season one's 'Tigh Me Up, Tigh Me Down'. "I had a wonderful time directing 'Taking a Break'," Olmos says. "It was a very different kind of storytelling from my first episode. I found it really provocative. We got to deal with issues of torture and the resolution of commitment between couples.

"I thought the episode turned out very well," he notes. "It was very strong."

'Taking a Break From All Your Worries' proved equally memorable for James Callis. "I thought that was a watershed episode for Baltar," Callis explains. "The very first thing Gaius tries to do is kill himself. That's been a long time coming. Finally, he's driven to that point because of his guilt and, in some perverse sense, compassion. It's a selfless act of a selfish man. I also particularly enjoyed the scene where Baltar is interrogated by Gaeta; that was very interesting."

Gaeta's interrogation of Baltar culminates in the *Galactica* CIC officer attempting to murder the former President. "That's an explosive moment," Alessandro Juliani notes. "Gaeta reaches breaking point. It was great to do that scene. In a way, it felt like we were doing theatre — there I was doing long scenes with James, and the prison cell felt like a stage."

Another character who loses their cool in 'Taking a Break From All Your Worries' is President Roslin. Mary McDonnell credits the episode's director for allowing her to show new depths of Laura Roslin's rage and anger. "Eddie really encouraged me to push Laura's emotional boundaries in that episode," she explains. "The idea was that her anger would drive her actions, unlike the controlled Laura that we see so often. It was fascinating to explore that part of her and it was kind of a pleasure to unleash it — although I don't know if it was fun for James Callis!"

In addition to examining Roslin and Gaeta's hatred of Baltar, 'Taking a Break From All Your Worries' also directly addresses the ongoing mystery of whether Baltar is a Cylon, during his drug-fuelled interrogation by Roslin and Adama. This sequence was initially set to feature burned and bloodied adult survivors of the Twelve Colonies, but was subsequently revised to feature children. "That scene was very controversial, but it turned out great," Moore notes. "It also puts to bed in Baltar's mind the possibility that he might be a Cylon. He says he isn't, although he still doesn't really know."

SURVEILLANCE: ADDITIONAL

During Baltar's questioning by Gaeta, the former President whispers a comment into the ear of his former aide that provokes Gaeta to attack him. At one point in the episode's development, this moment was going to provide a cryptic reference to the Sagittaron massacre that was planned to be revealed in the season finale. "We discussed the idea that Baltar might threaten to implicate Gaeta in the massacre and that would push him over the edge and make Gaeta try to kill him," Ronald D. Moore explains. "But the moment still works without the Sagittaron plotline — I think the viewer still gets the idea that Baltar is threatening to frame Gaeta in some way and implicate him as a collaborator."

Above: Baltar accuses Gaeta of being a traitor — with painful results for the former President...

In-between torturing Baltar, 'Taking a Break From All Your Worries' sees Lee trying to save his marriage to Dualla. Kandyse McClure was grateful for the opportunity to explore and develop her character's relationship with her husband. "That was a beautiful and trying episode for me," McClure recalls. "We finally get to see Dualla unhinged and confronting Lee about their differences — and his love for Kara. I thought that it was important to show that Dualla knows Lee is in love with Kara but feels that she herself is also worthy of his love. That shows that Dualla values herself.

"The scene where Lee makes his heartfelt speech to Dualla was magic to play with Jamie," she notes. "I thought there was a quiet resonance to that scene."

McClure's feelings on the episode are echoed by her screen husband, who feels that its revised storyline was far more effective than the original, lighter plot. "'Taking a Break From All Your Worries' turned out to be one of my favourite episodes of the season," Bamber states. "Lee completely loses it in that episode. He's a mess — he doesn't know where he is or who he is meant to be any more. That was extremely interesting and rewarding for me to play.

"All in all, I love 'Taking a Break' and see this episode as the perfect example of why *Battlestar* works so well," he adds. "We are all allowed to contribute. We all care. And our show juxtaposes every aspect of life. In this case it is a study of betrayal in all its forms: intrapersonal, interpersonal and, on the grandest scale, political and even biological. That's quite an achievement for forty-four minutes of television." ∎

[THE WOMAN KING]

WRITER: Michael Angeli
DIRECTOR: Michael Rymer

GUEST CAST: Bruce Davison (Dr Micah Robert), Gabrielle Rose (Mrs King), Richard Hatch (Tom Zarek), Leah Cairns (Lieutenant Margaret 'Racetrack' Edmondson), Ryan Robbins (Charlie Connor), Colin Lawrence (Hamish 'Skulls' McCall), Chris Boyd (Cheadle), Colin Corringan (Nowart), Lily Duong-Walton (Hera Agathon)

"This guy's dirty. I think he's a liar and I think he's killing people because he's a racist son-of-a-bitch." — Karl 'Helo' Agathon

Mellorak Sickness is spreading among the Sagittaron refugees housed in the *Galactica* hangar deck dubbed 'Dogsville' — but the majority of its occupants are refusing medical treatment, due to their religious beliefs. When the Sagittaron Willie King dies after being treated by Dr Micah Robert, the young man's mother tells the "Mayor of Dogsville", Lieutenant Karl 'Helo' Agathon, that her son was just one of the Sagittarons poisoned by Robert.

Helo expresses his concerns about Robert to Admiral Adama, much to the anger of Dr Robert's friend, Saul Tigh. Tigh warns Helo not to spread unfounded allegations, but Agathon refuses to drop the matter — even after his daughter, Hera, is successfully treated by Robert.

Desperate to expose Dr Robert's racist actions, Helo breaks into the *Galactica*'s medical records and discovers evidence that ninety per cent of the Sagittarons the physician treated on New Caprica died. Doc Cottle dismisses Helo's claim, but later performs an autopsy on Willie King's body and discovers that Robert injected him with a toxin. After Robert is arrested for his crimes, Admiral Adama apologizes to Helo for not taking his claims more seriously.

"'The Woman King' was very exciting for me, because it was the first Helo episode," says Tahmoh Penikett. "When I read the script, I thought it was a great storyline and a terrific opportunity for me. It was the script I had been waiting three years for — and I can't thank the producers enough for it."

The premise for 'The Woman King' was conceived by writer Michael Angeli, in response to a request from the Sci Fi Channel. "At that point, we had burned up all of our stories and we got a mandate from the network to do some stand-alone episodes," Angeli recalls. "I had always wanted to do a story that involved forced euthanasia and the idea of creating a superior race, so that was my starting point for the storyline.

"I also knew I wanted to do a story with Helo," he continues. "I like Tahmoh Penikett a lot, I think there's something extremely subtle in his craft, and I felt he had

Opposite: Academy Award-nominated actor Bruce Davison was cast in 'The Woman King' because of his ability to play Helo's antagonist, Dr Micah Robert, as "a plausible good guy".

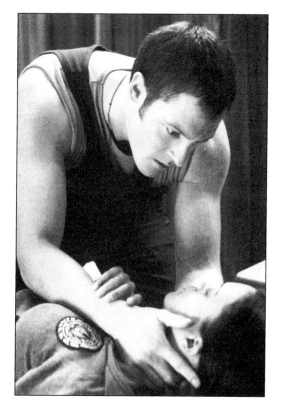

been under-used in the show. I also felt there was an opportunity to follow-up events in 'A Measure of Salvation'; the idea is that Helo has been put in charge of Dogsville because Adama knew he had killed the Cylons in that earlier episode."

As Angeli's premise took shape, it became clear to the series' makers that the episode could feature the Sagittarons — and begin the planned multi-episode Sagittaron storyline that was set to culminate in the revelation of the Sagittaron massacre during Baltar's season-ending trial. The threat to the Sagittarons' continued existence was then generated by the combination of a disease and a prejudiced, Sagittaron-hating doctor, Micah Robert.

"The allegorical value of the story was quite high," director Michael Rymer notes. "I initially sort of joked about it being the Alan Alda show — it's the 'Let's make a liberal statement: racism is bad' show. But I ultimately think we found a way to do it a little more subtly than that — the episode isn't just about people being racist, it's about how when good men fail to act, people perish."

Rymer was thrilled when Academy Award-nominated character actor Bruce Davison (of *X-Men*, *Short Cuts* and *Longtime Companion* fame) signed up to play the malicious medicine man. "The key to casting the doctor was to find somebody who was a plausible good guy, a real person who had his own point of view," Rymer explains. "When people perform acts of ethnic cleansing, they believe in what they're doing — they're not saying to themselves, maybe I can do this dastardly deed and get away with it. And that's what Bruce got across well. I thought he did an excellent job as Helo's antagonist."

Canadian actress Gabrielle Rose played the titular role of Mrs King. Another prolific performer, Rose's many credits include the Steven Spielberg-produced miniseries *Taken*, *The Sweet Hereafter* and the Mark Verheiden-scripted 1994 movie *TimeCop*. "I thought Gabrielle Rose was a really good choice," Tahmoh Penikett notes. "She's a really talented actress and it was great to do some intense emotional scenes with her. We'd actually worked together before on a Tori Spelling film [the 2005 movie *Hush*]."

Helo's willingness to investigate Mrs King's claims drives a wedge between him and his crewmates — especially Colonel Tigh. Tigh's criticism of Agathon's actions earns him a punch in the face from Helo, in a confrontation that both Penikett and Michael Hogan were thrilled to shoot.

"I thought it was fun to see Helo and Tigh go head to head," Hogan notes. "I don't have much to do with Helo normally, so I was pleased to get to do that scene. Tahmoh's a neat guy to work with."

Helo's confrontation with Tigh was initially conceived to open the episode, which would then have continued by flashing back to the events that led to their argument. This idea was abandoned in favour of a more traditional narrative structure, at the request of Michael Rymer. "That's my big problem with the episode," Angeli reveals. "I felt opening with the confrontation between Tigh and Helo gave the episode intrigue and left the viewer wanting to know what had happened to get them there. But Michael Rymer wanted to play it without the time jump, so we changed it. Personally, I felt that undercut the piece, although Michael did a great job shooting the episode."

Another key element of Angeli's script that didn't make the final cut was a scene in which Helo confessed to Adama that he had been responsible for killing the Cylons in 'A Measure of Salvation'. "I liked that scene a lot," Ronald D. Moore says. "I have mixed feelings about whether we should have cut it. It wasn't just cut for time; we cut it because it didn't go anywhere. Helo told Adama and that was it. But one of the reasons for doing the episode in the first place was to address the aftermath of Helo's actions and that was the one scene that directly did that. So in that regard, it was an important scene."

Moore has similarly mixed feelings about the episode as a whole. "I was disappointed with certain aspects of it," he notes. "The episode doesn't say anything new. It says racism is bad, which is not a new or provocative message. I also felt the relationship between Helo and the woman King should have been richer and more interesting, and I don't feel the Sagittarons really emerge as a unique culture in the show. The racial animosity people like Tigh and Tyrol show towards the Sagittarons seems to come out of nowhere, too — we've never shown anything like that before.

"But there were also a lot of things I liked in the show," he continues. "I felt the episode explored things like Helo's life on the ship and his self-image really effectively. I also liked the way we used Doc Cottle. It was interesting to see him lie about the

Opposite: 'The Woman King' was devised as a Helo-centred episode that followed-up from events in 'A Measure of Salvation'.

autopsy just because he's tired and doesn't want to deal with something. It's a small character thing but it's totally believable, because human beings sometimes lie for stupid reasons. So, overall, I'd say it's a good episode."

Angeli's verdict on the finished episode is similarly balanced. "If you look at the bulletin boards, 'The Woman King' doesn't seem to be as popular as many of the other episodes in season three," Angeli points out. "But I think it achieved what it was supposed to achieve: it was a cool self-contained story about Helo being the boy who cried wolf. I also think Tahmoh did a great job with it." ∎

SURVEILLANCE: ADDITIONAL

The planned B-plot for 'The Woman King' focused on Tom Zarek's unhappiness at plans for Gaius Baltar to stand trial. This B-plot was designed to pave the way for the season-ending revelations about the Sagittaron massacre on New Caprica, and saw Zarek visiting Baltar in prison and telling the former President he would be spared the death sentence if he pleaded guilty. On hearing Zarek's offer, the Number Six that resides in Baltar's mind realized that Zarek wasn't concerned about Baltar's well-being at all, but feared Baltar would reveal details of his involvement in the Sagittaron massacre on the stand. Baltar then rejected Zarek's offer.

"We dropped that B-plot when we changed our plans for Baltar's trial in the finale," Ronald D. Moore explains. "But the loss of that B-plot didn't really harm the episode at all."

[A DAY IN THE LIFE]

WRITER: Mark Verheiden
DIRECTOR: Rod Hardy

GUEST CAST: Lucinda Jenney (Carolanne Adama), Jennifer Halley (Seelix), Don Thompson (Anthony Figurski), Bodie Olmos (Lieutenant Brendan 'Hotdog' Costanza), Sebastian Spence (Lieutenant Noel 'Narcho' Allison), Finn Devit (Nicholas Tyrol), Michael Leisen (Private Stuart Jaffee)

> **"I knew you long before you were the Admiral. Back when you were just Bill. The husband who wasn't there. The father who left. Just Bill."**
> **— Carolanne Adama, to William Adama**

Forty-nine days after the last Cylon sighting, Admiral Adama marks his wedding anniversary by recalling his life and troubled relationship with his long-dead ex-wife, Carolanne. When he discusses his decision to leave Carolanne with his son Lee, Adama is shocked to learn that his former wife became an abusive alcoholic — and that his two sons hated him for leaving them with her.

As plans for Gaius Baltar's trial take shape, a malfunction leaves Chief Tyrol and Cally trapped in an airlock with a rapidly depleting oxygen supply. After every attempt to open the airlock fails, Admiral Adama orders a Raptor team to blast open the space-side airlock door and then retrieve Tyrol and Cally before they are lost into the vacuum of space. Narrowly surviving the operation, Tyrol later promises Cally that their lives together will be better in the days ahead…

The core premise of 'A Day in the Life' had been discussed as a possible *Battlestar Galactica* storyline for more than a year before the episode's production. "Ron Moore had wanted to do an Adama episode along these lines for as long as I'd been on the show," explains writer Mark Verheiden, who joined the series at the start of its second season. "The question was always, 'What story do we want to tell about Adama's earlier life and how does that impact the Admiral on *Galactica*?'"

After previously planning (and, ultimately, abandoning) an Adama flashback episode as the season two première, Moore invited Verheiden to develop a storyline that combined flashbacks to Adama's past with a character study of his daily life on *Galactica*. "I liked the concept of doing a day in a life episode and centring it around Adama," Moore explains. "I was also interested in getting to know the woman Adama was married to, but never talks about. I fell in love with this idea that Adama allows himself to think about her just one day a year, on their wedding anniversary. There was something sweet and poetic about that."

This concept was combined with a B-plot in which Tyrol and Cally find themselves

Opposite: William Adama re-examines his relationship with his former wife Carolanne in 'A Day in the Life'.

Above: Moore feels that the episode's B-plot — Tyrol and Cally's fight for survival — was more effective than its main storyline.

facing death as a result of a seemingly simple airlock repair mission they are assigned by Adama during his 'average day'. "We wanted to show that there's no such thing as a 'casual order' on a warship," Verheiden notes. "Tyrol and Cally find themselves almost dying, not in battle, not against the Cylons, but simply trying to do some routine maintenance. I really wanted to get back to the idea that space is an unforgiving, inhospitable and uniquely dangerous environment, even without Cylons."

While writing the episode's script, Verheiden drew on ideas previously established by the show as well as Moore's Series Bible. "We knew Adama had been married and divorced, and we knew Lee had a chip on his shoulder about his old man," he explains. "Early on, Ron suggested a spin on Lee's attitude, one that became the driving force for the Adama back-story. Lee wasn't mad at Adama for leaving him, but because he left Lee and Zak with Carolanne, who was hardly the idealized 'perfect Mom' Adama had conjured up in his mind. Carolanne was a woman with significant problems, which is why Adama divorced her in the first place. So the story became an exploration of both Adama's idealized version of her, and of him coming to terms finally with the darker reality."

The revelations about Carolanne Adama surprised *Battlestar Galactica*'s leading man, Edward James Olmos. "That episode was a real eye-opener," Olmos says. "I didn't know that Adama's wife had been an alcoholic or that she had treated his children badly. They were interesting developments."

The pivotal role of Carolanne Adama was won by Lucinda Jenney, a prolific character actress whose credits range from the movies *Rain Man*, *Thelma & Louise* and *Leaving Las Vegas* to the TV shows *24*, *Carnivale* and *The Shield*. In helming Jenney's scenes with Olmos, one of the biggest challenges faced by returning *Battlestar Galactica* director Rod Hardy was finding a way to make their characters' interaction distinct from Baltar's visions of Number Six.

"In early versions of the storyline, we

SURVEILLANCE: ADDITIONAL

'A Day in the Life' paves the way for Lee Adama's involvement with Baltar's trial. "Lee's interest in the law might seem a little awkward because it effectively comes out of nowhere, but I think you have to allow a TV show to invent things about a character as it develops," says Ronald D. Moore of this plot thread. "So I feel this is a perfectly acceptable thing for us to do — and it's something that pays off really well at the end of the season."

planned to show Carolanne the same way as we show Number Six interacting with Baltar," Moore explains. "But we needed to distinguish that from those visions, because we didn't want people to think Carolanne was supposed to be a Cylon. We talked about various alternatives, but in the end Eddie and the director settled on the idea of Adama repeatedly imagining himself with Carolanne at their home, rather than having her wander around the ship with him."

The Adama home was actually a real house in north Vancouver. "We looked at several different homes, some of which were starker and more realistic in terms of what a younger officer might have on Caprica, but the producers wanted an idealized/idyllic place that plays to Adama's initial memories of his wife," production designer Richard Hudolin says of the location's selection. "We made it more comfortable and cosy by doing things like bringing in some extra plants, which provides a contrast to Adama's world on the *Galactica*."

The B-plot of 'A Day in the Life' sees Adama leading the rescue mission of Tyrol and Cally. These scenes gave Aaron Douglas and Nicki Clyne a chance to explore their characters' troubled relationship and also required them to don harnesses for the sequence in which Tyrol and Cally are propelled into space.

"That episode was really great to shoot," says Nicki Clyne. "I had a lot to do and a lot to focus on. I thought the scene where Cally tells Adama who should care for her son was very moving and the whole scenario was very frightening."

"It was amazing stuff," Douglas agrees. "It was great drama. It was also fun to work with Nicki for a bunch of days and be a bit silly at times."

Moore points to Tyrol and Cally's plight as the most powerful and emotional aspect of 'A Day in the Life'. But he also feels that this B-plot has more importance in the episode than it actually should. "I think we leaned towards the Cally and Tyrol storyline far more than was appropriate," he says. "It was always designed to be a small story, because a day in the life episode shouldn't be too dramatic — it's about a typical day and the minutiae of a character's life. But I think we started to move towards the Tyrol and Cally storyline, because of the problems in the Adama storyline. The Adama-Carolanne story just doesn't fire on all cylinders and the episode doesn't tell us that much about Adama and his daily life that we don't already know.

"Overall, I thought this episode was a bit of a misfire," Moore admits. "It just doesn't do justice to, or even stay true to, its premise."

Moore's disappointment with 'A Day in the Life' is shared, to some extent, by Mark Verheiden. "While I'm pleased with the episode, it's also a little frustrating because I think it could have landed harder," he states. "But overall, I think it was an interesting exploration of the Admiral's past. Any time we can focus on Edward Olmos that's a good thing." ■

SURVEILLANCE: ADDITIONAL

During the development of season three's Cylon Basestar story arc, the writing staff did discuss showing Baltar on an elevated command chair as an homage to the original series. "We talked about that every once and a while," Ronald D. Moore reveals, "but I never found any plausible explanation for why he would have any position of authority over there. So it never quite fit into the mythos of our show."

[DIRTY HANDS]

WRITERS: Jane Espenson & Anne Cofell Saunders
DIRECTOR: Wayne Rose

GUEST CAST: David Patrick Green (Xeno Fenner), Jerry Wasserman (Cabott), Samuel Patrick Chu (Milo), Jennifer Halley (Seelix), Leah Cairns (Lieutenant Margaret 'Racetrack' Edmondson), Colin Lawrence (Ensign Hamish 'Skulls' McCall), Samantha Ferris (Pollux), Wesley Salter (Redford)

"This plant is off-line. We're on strike!" — Chief Galen Tyrol

After a batch of contaminated Tylium fuel causes a Raptor to collide with Colonial One, Admiral Adama orders Chief Tyrol to investigate the incident. Tyrol discovers that the people aboard the Tylium ship have become discontent with their harsh working conditions and are threatening to sabotage fuel production in protest of their treatment.

Although this protest is quickly stopped by the arrest of the workers' leaders, Tyrol finds himself increasingly troubled by President Roslin's suppression of workers' rights and the observations about the Colonial class struggle contained in Gaius Baltar's political manifesto, *My Triumphs, My Mistakes*. The former union leader's campaign for better working conditions results in him calling a general strike aboard the Tylium ship.

Concerned by the danger the strike poses to the survival of the fleet, Adama forces Tyrol to order the Tylium miners back to work by threatening to execute the striking Deck Gang — starting with Cally. But after Tyrol ends the strike, Adama arranges a collective bargaining meeting between President Roslin and the reformed Colonial Workers' Alliance, as represented by Tyrol. Their first session leads to Colonial workers gaining several concessions — including Seelix's acceptance into the Officer Flight Training programme.

Before it became a Chief Tyrol showcase, 'Dirty Hands' began life as 'Our Enemies, Ourselves', a Dualla-focused episode that continued the Sagittaron storyline started by 'The Woman King'. "The episode was originally about Dualla having to represent the government in its dealings with the Sagittarons," reveals Ronald D. Moore. "In the story, Dualla was initially perceived by the Sagittarons as a traitor to her own people. But as the episode developed, she was then going to side with the Sagittarons against Adama, until Adama gave them their own ship at the end of the episode.

"There were interesting ideas in the episode but it was a difficult script and in the end I said, 'Forget it, it's not working.'" Moore continues. "We then decided to focus on the class issues that were in the original script and make the episode about labor, the class struggle and the need for unions."

As Chief Tyrol was an obvious central character for a union-themed episode, the show's writers knew they would have to make 'Dirty Hands' before the shocking revelation of the season finale, 'Crossroads, Part II'. "We had decided Tyrol was going to be a Cylon right around the time I was working on 'Our Enemies, Ourselves'," Anne Cofell Saunders explains. "Ron said we weren't going to get another shot to tell this union story about Tyrol. We knew that once he was revealed as a Cylon, we wouldn't be able to tell such a small, human story about his roots."

'Our Enemies, Ourselves' had originally been scheduled to follow 'The Woman King' in season three's production and airing order, but the episode was moved behind 'A Day in the Life' to enable its transformation into 'Dirty Hands'. Due to the tight time constraints involved, freelancer Jane Espenson was asked to deliver the episode's script, following her successful work on the earlier season three instalment 'The Passage'.

"Ron and the staff had come up with a basic storyline for 'Dirty Hands', which they needed turned into a script very quickly," Espenson recalls. "I wrote the script, which preserved some elements of what Anne had written. Anne was also my shepherd on the project — I called on her several times for guidance and advice. One idea that came from my general direction had to do with Tyrol's opinion on an issue being influenced by him having a young son. That ended up sticking."

'Dirty Hands' had been earmarked for director Wayne Rose during season three's mid-season production hiatus. After helming the *Battlestar Galactica* web series 'The Resistance' and serving as a first assistant director and second unit director on the main series, Rose was thrilled to finally helm an episode.

"There had been talk of me directing an episode since the second season and I was so excited to actually get one," says Rose, whose previous directorial credits included episodes of *Cleopatra 2525* and *Jack of All Trades*. "I was a bit concerned by the storyline, because it was a linear, single storyline that doesn't tie into the mythos. But Tyrol is such a strong character that he really carries the episode."

Tyrol's role at the heart of the action was similarly welcomed by Aaron Douglas, who enjoyed

Above: Galen Tyrol became the star of the workers' union-themed episode 'Dirty Hands' after the planned Sagittaron-focused storyline 'Our Enemies, Ourselves' was abandoned just prior to entering production.

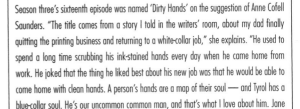

SURVEILLANCE: ADDITIONAL

Season three's sixteenth episode was named 'Dirty Hands' on the suggestion of Anne Cofell Saunders. "The title comes from a story I told in the writers' room, about my dad finally quitting the printing business and returning to a white-collar job," she explains. "He used to spend a long time scrubbing his ink-stained hands every day when he came home from work. He joked that the thing he liked best about his new job was that he would be able to come home with clean hands. A person's hands are a map of their soul — and Tyrol has a blue-collar soul. He's our uncommon common man, and that's what I love about him. Jane immediately jumped on the concept — so that's the title!"

Above: James Callis wasn't convinced by the revelation of Gaius Baltar's humble origins. "I just didn't add up for me," he says.

seeing Tyrol resume his career as a union leader. "I loved 'Dirty Hands'," says Douglas. "It shows an intellectual side of the Chief. He negotiates for the little man — he sits down with Adama and Roslin to argue his case — and he comes out on the right side of things.

"I had a great experience doing 'Dirty Hands'. It was the first time I worked every day on an episode. I felt extremely grateful to the writers for that script and I enjoyed working with Wayne Rose, who's such a terrific director. I also particularly enjoyed my scenes with Mary McDonnell."

Douglas' enthusiasm for 'Dirty Hands' is shared by President Roslin's real-life alterego. "I really liked that episode," explains Mary McDonnell. "I loved working with Aaron and I enjoyed the break from the bigger issues of the Cylons and the war. I liked exploring how the President dealt with the head of the union — and seeing how comfortable she seemed doing that."

One of the episode's most shocking moments concerns Admiral Adama's threat to execute the striking Cally. This moment was a result of Moore's desire for added complexity in the storytelling. "I wanted Adama to make the point that you can't have people disobeying orders on a warship in a time of war," he explains. "Adama's threat to shoot Cally is a shocking moment, but it's also very believable."

Tyrol's campaign for workers' rights is inspired by the harsh conditions aboard the Tylium mining ship. The scenes set aboard the ship were actually shot at Rogers Sugar, the Vancouver sugar refinery which previously doubled as parts of Ragnar Station in the *Battlestar Galactica* miniseries. "That was a great location," Rose notes. "We shot there on Halloween day and it was really cold and tough going. But it looks great on screen, so it was well worth it."

Much of Gaius Baltar's role in 'Dirty Hands' was inspired by scenes in 'Our Enemies, Ourselves'. The earlier script introduced the idea that Baltar had been writing a *Mein Kampf*-style political manifesto and showed him being visited by Dualla. It also established that Baltar had changed his accent to disguise his real background — which was originally going to be Sagittaron (as established by Moore's Series Bible), but was later shifted to the Aerilon town of Cuttlesbreath Wash. "I always loved the idea for that scene," Moore says. "I liked the way it gives the viewer something unexpected about the character."

After discussing various regional British accents with David Eick (including Eick's favoured Michael Caine-style Cockney and a Devon brogue), James Callis agreed to draw on his years studying at York University and employ a Yorkshire accent as Baltar's natural dialect. But he also made it clear to Eick before shooting the scene that he wasn't convinced this particular revelation was a good idea.

"The idea of a poor boy made good is very interesting, but it shouldn't have been given to Gaius Baltar," Callis explains. "I felt it was really odd, because if Baltar was trying so hard to sound like someone from Caprica, how come he's the only character on the show with an English accent? Was his elocution teacher deaf? It just didn't add up for me. I was concerned people would think I'd gone mad. I just didn't think it was a smart move. But the producers loved the idea, so that's why we did it."

Moore is happy to address Callis' criticism. "You can get into a whole argument of accents and him being British, but I don't think it's important to the drama or what it says about the character," Moore argues. "Baltar is accepted as someone from Caprica — that's all you need to know."

The combination of Baltar's revelation about his past with Tyrol's fight for better workers' rights made 'Dirty Hands' one of season three's more effective stand-alone episodes in Moore's eyes. "I like the episode because it addresses important issues and delves into life in the fleet in a way many episodes don't," he states. "I know it's the political polemic I always said our series wouldn't be — I always said our show would ask questions without giving answers — but I support the message of the episode and the way it reminds people why unions exist. And I think it's an important episode because of that." ∎

SURVEILLANCE: ADDITIONAL

The shot of Chief Tyrol finding Baltar's book replaced an earlier scene in which Tyrol encountered two workers who were reading it while on duty. "The scene featured two extras who couldn't be directed — due to union rules, ironically," Ronald D. Moore recalls with a laugh. "As a result they were terrible, so we had to lose that scene."

Another change to the episode involved Roslin's search for the latest pages of Baltar's book. The scene was initially set to see Baltar being strip-searched naked for the pages, but this was changed at the actors' request. "I really wanted them to do it," Moore says. "But the actors felt they wanted to preserve a bit of Baltar's dignity."

[MAELSTROM]

WRITERS: David Weddle & Bradley Thompson
DIRECTOR: Michael Nankin

GUEST CAST: Dorothy Lyman (Socrata Thrace), Callum Keith Rennie (Leoben Conoy), Georgia Craig (Oracle Brenn), Erika-Shaye Gair (Child Kara), Don Thompson (Anthony Figurski), Leah Cairns (Lieutenant Margaret 'Racetrack' Edmondson), Bodie Olmos (Lieutenant Brendan 'Hotdog' Costanza)

"Momma, something's about to happen. And I think you were trying to prepare me for it..." — Kara Thrace

While the fleet refuels near the stormy atmosphere of a planet, Kara Thrace sees a Cylon raider lurking in the dense clouds and pursues it. Following a dogfight the ship suddenly disappears — and Kara is later shocked to learn there is no evidence of the Raider's existence.

Admiral Adama considers grounding Kara, but Lee decides to keep her on active duty. Kara begins to question her own sanity, however, as she finds herself haunted by visions of her past — including her captivity on New Caprica and her earlier life with her abusive mother, Socrata Thrace.

After recalling how her mother died alone, Kara experiences a vision in which she is encouraged to face her mother's death by Leoben. In the wake of the experience, Kara realizes that her guide is actually a mysterious entity merely assuming the Cylon's guise. She then attempts to seize her destiny — by propelling her Viper towards a mysterious vortex in the planet's atmosphere that resembles the mandala from her visions. Lee can only watch in horror as Kara's Viper explodes...

It was destined to contain one of the most shocking developments in *Battlestar Galactica*'s history — but 'Maelstrom' was not originally built around the mysterious demise of one of the series' most beloved characters. "The death of Starbuck was not planned far in advance," reveals David Weddle, co-writer of 'Maelstrom'. "The idea, like most of our best ones, grew organically from the events we had created in previous episodes."

'Maelstrom' was initially set to be a 'viper combat show' in the spirit of Weddle and Thompson's earlier scripts for 'Act of Contrition' and 'Scar'. The episode's original outline propelled Starbuck and Apollo into a lengthy battle with a Cylon Heavy Raider.

"David Eick initially proposed the episode as a 'Dogfight in the Dark', somewhere in a planetary fog, where Kara and Lee have chased a Heavy Raider," Thompson recalls. "They get trapped below the hard deck and cannot regain orbit. In the few moments before they're pulled down to where the increasing atmospheric pressures will crush them, they must confront their feelings for each other. It turns out there's a tech solution for their dilemma, but it involves one pilot's certain death to save the other. Kara was going to choose to die to save Lee, but somehow Lee managed to pull her out. That was the gist of what we first sent to the network."

The premise for 'Maelstrom' began to take a different direction, however, after Katee Sackhoff quizzed Weddle about the significance of the mandala on the Temple of Five in 'Rapture' and asked how it related to the painting in Kara's apartment shown in 'Valley of Darkness'. When Weddle told her that the writing staff hadn't actually finalized the meaning of events, Sackhoff expressed her hope that Kara would somehow encounter Leoben again in another round of their ongoing psychodrama and would learn about her past and special destiny.

"The writing staff decided to follow Katee's lead," Weddle says. "We began outlining a show in which Kara is abducted by Leoben, who subjects her to a drug-induced *Manchurian Candidate*-style brainwashing psychodrama that forces her to revisit events in her past and see them in a new light. When Ron Moore came in I was in a cold sweat, because we had gone in a radically different direction, but Ron didn't even blink. He went with it."

While the new storyline involved Kara resisting Leoben's psychological torture and ultimately gaining a new clue about the whereabouts of Earth, Moore responded to their pitch by casually suggesting an addition. "Ron came up with the idea of Kara flying into a cloud that resembled the mandala in her painting and her ship blowing up," Weddle reveals. "When he first told us that idea, we all blinked in astonishment. 'You mean you want to kill Kara?' Ron shrugged, 'Why not? Let's try it and see what happens.'"

Above: 'Maelstrom' naturally developed into a pivotal episode for Kara Thrace after Katee Sackhoff asked for a storyline that explored her character's past and special destiny.

"I liked the initial story but I didn't think it hit you in the face as much as I wanted," Moore explains. "So I said, 'The truth is, we should just kill her.' From then on, I fell in love with the idea of killing off Starbuck, and bringing her back later in the series. I loved the audacity of the idea and sensed the death of Starbuck would propel us forward in the overall storyline of the show and take us to the next chapter."

Weddle and Thompson began to develop the

other aspects of the episode's plotline with Moore. The writers quickly decided that Kara's exploration of her past and secret destiny would be driven by her reevaluation of her relationship with her mother and her death — and that 'Leoben' would convince Kara to come to terms with her mother's loss, in preparation for her own death. "Ron was very clear that the focus of the drama would be Leoben convincing her to kill herself, so she could embrace her destiny," Weddle says. "And that Leoben would turn out not to be Leoben at all, but a mysterious presence that took the form of Leoben."

In response to director Michael Nankin's initial comments that he didn't fully understand Kara's issues with her mother, Weddle and Thompson developed the idea that Socrata Thrace was aware of her daughter's special destiny and was trying to give her the strength to fulfil it, albeit in a twisted way.

After learning of her character's death (and planned return) from Moore and David Eick, Katee Sackhoff aimed to give Kara Thrace a memorable send-off in 'Maelstrom'. "I put myself out there, as an actress, more than I had ever done in my life, for that episode," Sackhoff explains. "I knew I was going out — for a while, anyway — so I wanted to go out with a bang. I wanted it to be my best work on the show."

Sackhoff's highlights of working on 'Maelstrom' included acting alongside prolific TV actress Dorothy Lyman (*All My Children, Another World, Mama's Family*) as Kara's mother. "Dorothy Lyman was amazing to work with," Sackhoff says. "Our scenes together are heartbreaking. They were hard to do.

"The whole episode was just really challenging to shoot, because my character finally comes to terms with her mother, herself and her own demons," she notes. "It was hard to put yourself in a position where you feel you've come to terms with who you are and everything you've accomplished in life — and feel you're ready to pursue your destiny."

'Maelstrom' was also challenging for Callum Keith Rennie, as it required him to play a mysterious character who was merely assuming the form of Leoben. "I really liked that episode, but it was confusing for me at times," Rennie recalls. "One minute I'd be doing dark moments, and the next thing I knew I'd be playing this gentle guide, who is guiding Starbuck into her past and helping her deal with her issues."

Jamie Bamber savoured his character's interaction with Kara Thrace in this episode, which was designed to bring their relationship full circle. "I had a fantastic time," Bamber says. "At that point, Lee and Kara are old friends with scars that have healed, or maybe still hurt a bit. Essentially, they have a brother/sister-type relationship.

"There was something really engaging about Lee trying to protect and help this woman who is falling apart, and protect her in the wrong way — by giving her duties and responsibilities that end up killing her," he notes. "It was a big pay-off for

SURVEILLANCE: ADDITIONAL

Dirk Benedict's Starbuck is killed and resurrected in the original *Battlestar Galactica* two-parter 'War of the Gods'. The character's return was facilitated by advanced, god-like aliens who inhabited a Ship of Lights. When asked about the similarities between the original Starbuck's fate and Kara Thrace's death and return in season three, Moore has to be reminded of the original series storyline before responding. "Now that you mention it, I do remember that," he reveals. "But no, it was not something we'd talked about when we were doing 'Maelstrom'. It never came up and had no bearing on that episode."

everything that had happened in the season."

In an attempt to keep their plans for Kara's return a surprise, Moore and Eick initially asked Sackhoff to pretend she believed she had been dropped from the series. Unfortunately, a few days after the script for 'Maelstrom' had been released, Moore learned that the mood on set had taken a dive and decided to share their plans with selected members of the cast and crew.

As the initial controversy over Sackhoff's apparent exit died down, Edward James Olmos established the desired tone on set by shooting his character's response to Starbuck's death ahead of the other actors. Olmos also improvised the powerful climactic scene in which Admiral Adama destroys his model ship — which was actually one of two expensive prop ships the production had purchased at the start of the weekly series.

"It's a great moment," art director Douglas McLean recalls, "and it just shows how good Eddie's instincts are for where the scene is leading his character."

"David and I were watching when they shot that," Bradley Thompson adds. "We were in tears when Mr Olmos walked off the set afterwards — and not because the ship was broken. David and I were stunned and awed."

The genuine emotion on set clearly helped 'Maelstrom' fulfil its destiny to become one of season three's most exceptional episodes. "Watching Michael Nankin, Katee and the rest of the extraordinary cast and production team bring the pages Brad and I had written to life was breathtaking," David Weddle states. "I will never forget it. And it holds great personal meaning to me because Kara's relationship with her mother echoed many of the dynamics that I had with my father, who was also a marine and combat veteran."

"'Maelstrom' is a landmark episode for the series," Moore declares. "I think everyone did an amazing job on it." ∎

Above: Socrata Thrace's death scene was influenced by David Weddle's memory of his father's death. "I was with my father when he died," Weddle explains. "It turned out to be one of the most profound experiences of my life. The death of a parent forces you to come to terms with your own death. So I think some of that is reflected in the episode."

[THE SON ALSO RISES]

WRITER: Michael Angeli
DIRECTOR: Robert Young

GUEST CAST: Mark Sheppard (Romo Lampkin), Ty Olsson (Captain Aaron Kelly), Leah Cairns (Lieutenant Margaret 'Racetrack' Edmondson), Sebastian Spence (Lieutenant Noel 'Narcho' Allison), Don Thompson (Anthony Figurski), Colin Lawrence (Hamish 'Skulls' McCall), Tyler McClendon (Alan Hughes), Bodie Olmos (Lieutenant Brendan 'Hotdog' Costanza)

"There is no greater ally, no force more powerful, no enemy more resolved, than a son who chooses to step from his father's shadow."
— Romo Lampkin

Following the murder of Gaius Baltar's lawyer, Lee Adama is assigned to protect his replacement attorney — Romo Lampkin. A protégé of Joseph Adama, Lampkin intrigues the still-in-mourning Lee with his provocative view of humankind and the questionable tactics he employs in pursuit of justice. Lampkin's first achievements on becoming Baltar's attorney include manipulating Caprica Six into agreeing not to testify against her former lover.

After saving Lampkin from two assassination attempts, Lee discovers evidence that leads to the bomber — Captain Kelly. Following Kelly's confession, Lee tells his father he does not wish to resume his role as CAG but instead wishes to continue working with Lampkin during the trial. Admiral Adama reluctantly agrees to his son's request and prepares to serve as a judge on Baltar's trial, after he is selected from a lottery of fleet commanders...

'The Son Also Rises' was conceived to be the episode that paved the way for Gaius Baltar's trial in season three's two-part finale. "The episode sets up everything for the finale — it's essentially part one of a three-part storyline," Ronald D. Moore notes. "It establishes the legal system that we see in action in the finale, by putting in place the idea that ship commanders have been dealing with the enforcement of justice in the fleet. We also set up which of our characters will be participating in the trial.

"As we approached Baltar's trial, we always knew we wanted our characters to be involved.

SURVEILLANCE: ADDITIONAL

Michael Angeli's decision to name Gaius Baltar's lawyer Romo Lampkin was the subject of intense debate among *Battlestar Galactica*'s two executive producers. "The name was funny," Angeli recalls with a grin. "I knew Ron Moore and David Eick would both think I named it after them.

"Romo is the first two letters of Ron and the first two letters of Moore, and that's really where the name comes from. But David Eick is a huge Dallas Cowboys football fan and their quarterback is Tony Romo, so when he saw the name he emailed me and said, 'You named him for the Dallas Cowboys. That's cool!' I was like, 'Yeah, yeah!'"

We didn't want it to focus on guest stars. So we talked about Lee becoming Baltar's attorney and initially settled on the idea that Lee would assume that role after Baltar's original lawyer was killed. We then realized that was too much and decided to make Lee the lawyer's assistant. We also talked about Adama being one of the judges, after we considered making him the lone judge. I thought that would be interesting, and a good way to revive the father-son conflict between Adama and Lee.

"We always knew that Lee and Adama's involvement in the trial was a bit of a stretch," he admits, "but we did try to keep everything as believable as possible. We talked about the real-life legal system a lot. But ultimately we did what we needed to do for the drama of the piece."

From the beginning, the plotline of 'The Son Also Rises' involved Baltar's lawyers being marked for assassination, in a scenario inspired by the real-life attacks on Saddam Hussein's defence team. The job of bringing that premise to life was assigned to writer Michael Angeli, who was given free reign in the creation of Baltar's main attorney, Romo Lampkin. "I told Ron I had an idea for this guy," Angeli recalls, "and Ron said, 'Whatever you want to do, go for it. Just make him as interesting and as unique as you can. Don't hold back.' I was very grateful to Ron for that.

"I loved the idea of Romo Lampkin being this enigmatic cool guy who enters into our world," he continues. "I have also always been intrigued by the idea of kleptomaniacs and why they steal things. They don't do it for the booty — there's a psychological reason for it. So I made Romo a kleptomaniac.

"Some of Romo's back-story actually comes from my family," Angeli reveals. "I wear dark glasses myself. I liked playing with the idea that when Romo tells the truth, he keeps his glasses on — but when he tells an outright lie, he takes his glasses off.

Above: 'The Son Also Rises' was designed to set up Lee Adama's involvement in the season-ending trial of Gaius Baltar.

That was great. And I gave him a cat because I hate cats and I thought, to have something to remind you of your wife, that you despise but you feel stuck with, was an interesting twist."

Moore credits Angeli for making Romo Lampkin "a surprising yet believable and fully realized character" and was equally impressed by his interaction with — and subtle manipulation of — Lee Adama. *Battlestar Galactica*'s head writer also liked how Angeli's ideas about Joseph Adama fitted in with the work that had been done on the proposed prequel series *Caprica* — even though, ironically, Angeli hadn't actually read *Caprica*'s pilot episode at the time of writing 'The Son Also Rises'. "All I knew was that Joseph Adama was a lawyer," Angeli admits with a laugh. "I guess Ron and I must be on the same wavelength if what I wrote fits with *Caprica*."

The pivotal role of Romo Lampkin was quickly earmarked for Mark Sheppard. An acclaimed British-born, LA-based character actor whose many credits include memorable guest appearances in *24*, *Firefly* and *The X-Files*, Sheppard had previously discussed playing a different role in *Battlestar Galactica*'s second season, but was unavailable at the time due to his work on the Michael Angeli-produced *Medium*.

"I was a huge fan of *Battlestar* from the start," Sheppard says, "and I got to know Ron Moore through one of my best friends, [former *Star Trek: The Next Generation* producer] Naren Shankar. Naren suggested it would be a good idea for Ron and I to meet, because Ron was having some issues with his wireless technology at home and he knew I could sort that out for him. So Ron and I became friends and I told him, 'I would love to play a Cylon if the opportunity ever came up.' We then talked about a possible role in season two, but that didn't work out. Some time after that, I was at a party with Ron and David Eick, and David told me about a trial that was coming up on the show and asked if I'd be interested in playing a role in that. I said 'sure', and the next thing I knew I was offered three episodes!

"When I read the script for 'The Son Also Rises', I could not believe my luck," he notes. "I thought the figure of Romo Lampkin was extraordinary — he's a character who has a huge impact on everyone around him. I just loved the role. It was written so brilliantly by Michael Angeli."

Angeli is quick to return Sheppard's compliment. "Mark was perfect for the role," Angeli says. "He has an incredible sense of dialogue and a remarkable memory. He really took the character and made it whole."

Romo Lampkin's introduction and the way it set up Lee Adama's involvement in Baltar's trial was warmly welcomed by Jamie Bamber. "Romo's arrival drives Lee to acknowledge there's a different side of his character that has never been allowed to flourish," Bamber

SURVEILLANCE: ADDITIONAL

Early versions of the plotline for 'The Son Also Rises' were more Lee Adama-centric and saw him interrogating Number Six as the *Galactica*'s command crew debated on whether the Cylon, as a machine, could take the witness stand. Lee and Anders were also set to fight in the wake of Kara's death, until this idea was dismissed as being "too expected" by Moore.

The bomber storyline similarly underwent several changes during the episode's development. "Initially, we were not going to reveal the bomber," Ronald D. Moore explains. "We talked about keeping him alive as a threat through Baltar's trial. But then we decided to reveal him and selected Captain Kelly. I liked that. I thought it was a very believable choice."

notes. "It's a side he might share with his grandfather — this man who got involved in the darker side of what people do to each other and defended the lowest of the low. Through that, Lee finds himself defending the most hated man in existence and discovers things about himself and the people around him. I thought that was very interesting.

"I was very excited to get to play that with James Callis and Mark Sheppard, because it was such a different dynamic. And, after four years of *Battlestar*, I'd barely shared a scene with James up to that point!"

Due to the performance-intensive nature of the episode, regular *Battestar Galactica* director Robert Young was a natural choice to helm 'The Son Also Rises'. Young's touch is particularly evident in the scene which sees Lampkin manipulating Number Six into agreeing not to testify against Baltar.

"I thought the idea of giving

Lampkin the ability to discuss things with Six on a very deep level was lovely," Sheppard notes. "Romo manipulates her using somebody else's pen — which he stole!"

Above: "Mark was perfect for the part," says writer/co-executive producer Michael Angeli of Mark Sheppard's casting as Romo Lampkin.

While the cast savored the rich drama and performance value of 'The Son Also Rises', not everyone was so enamored with Angeli's choice of a companion for Romo Lampkin. "Everyone hated the cat," Angeli recalls with a laugh. "Eddie Olmos was going to strangle me. He came up to me and said, 'Dude, you wrote a beautiful script, one of the best scripts ever written for the show, and you put that fucking cat in it! Why don't you take it out?' I said, 'Tell you what, humour me. If the cat can't hit his mark, I'll take it out.' But in the first scene with the cat, when he jumped on to the table, he did it perfectly. So the cat stayed!" ■

[CROSSROADS, PART I]

WRITER: Michael Taylor
DIRECTOR: Michael Rymer

GUEST CAST: Mark Sheppard (Romo Lampkin), Chelah Horsdal (Didi Cassidy), Ryan Robbins (Charlie Connor), Jennifer Halley (Diana Seelix), Keegan Connor Tracy (Young Woman), Susan Hogan (Captain Franks), William Samples (Tribunal Judge), Lily Duong-Walton (Hera Agathon), Alison Matthews (Karen Fallbrook), Colin Lawrence (Hamish 'Skulls' McCall), Leah Cairns (Lieutenant Margaret 'Racetrack' Edmondson), Bodie Olmos (Lieutenant Brenden 'Hotdog' Costanza)

"I will not serve under a man who questions my integrity."
— Lee Adama

"And I won't have an officer under my command who doesn't have any."
— Admiral Adama

The trial of Gaius Baltar begins with the former President of the Twelve Colonies of Kobol being accused of collaborating with the Cylons on New Caprica and contributing to the loss of 5,197 human lives. While public opinion is clearly against Baltar, Romo Lampkin eloquently argues that the trial is motivated by mob bloodlust and President Roslin's need for vengeance.

After discrediting Colonel Tigh's testimony by forcing him to reveal how he murdered Ellen Tigh, Lampkin manipulates Lee Adama into making President Roslin reveal she has started taking the vision-inducing drug chamalla extract again. Roslin justifies her actions with a shocking announcement — her cancer has returned. Stunned by his behavior, Admiral Adama angrily rebukes Lee — while Dualla walks out on him.

As Baltar's trial continues, Admiral Adama and Colonel Tigh learn that the Cylons have been secretly tracking their journey to the Ionian nebula for months. Several people aboard the *Galactica* also mysteriously begin to experience strange sights and sounds…

SURVEILLANCE: ADDITIONAL

Season three's closing two episodes do not feature the series' main title sequence or the introductory 'precap' (which briefly establishes the show's back-story prior to the teaser). "We were pressed for time," Ronald D. Moore explains, "and asked if we could do away with them, just to give us more time to tell the story." 'Crossroads, Part II' also runs five minutes longer than a standard episode of the series.

"We always knew we wanted to do the trial of Gaius Baltar," says Ronald D. Moore as he recalls the genesis of season three's two-part finale. "We just didn't know when we were going to do it. We originally talked about Baltar's trial taking place just after the escape from the algae planet [in 'Rapture']. But as we started talking about what the season finale would be, I started to fall in love with the idea of it being Baltar's trial.

"There was a lot of concern — both internally and from the network — about us doing Baltar's trial as the finale," Moore admits. "We had done a trial episode before in season one ['Litmus'] and the network was not convinced a trial episode was the best way to end the season. So I told the writers we had to make sure it worked.

"When I saw the first cut of the two-parter I said, 'We've done it!'," he adds with pride. "It's a legitimate, really dramatic trial show."

Scripting duties on the finale were divided between Michael Taylor and Mark Verheiden, who wrote the first and second parts of 'Crossroads' respectively. "It was the luck of the draw that Mark and I got to do the finale," Taylor recalls. "In one sense it was a privilege, but in another it was horrifying. It was tough to figure out all the elements that we had planned for the finale and I don't know if either of us felt like *Law & Order* writers who were happy scripting a courtroom drama. But as it turned out, I think the material was so rich and interesting that it just wrote itself."

"We spent a lot of time talking about legal terminology and tactics," Verheiden confirms. "Fortunately, we had a wonderful new character to play with in Romo Lampkin."

During the initial development of 'Crossroads', the writing staff intended to pay off the Sagittaron storyline which they had planned to set up in earlier episodes. Early versions of Part I's storyline climaxed with Lee Adama discovering what seemed to be damning evidence of Baltar's involvement in a massacre of Sagittarons on

Above: The Number Six in Baltar's head appears to him in his cell as he awaits his trial.

New Caprica. Part II would then have revealed the true context of this video footage, with the jury learning that Baltar was actually fighting to avert the massacre. As the finale was readied for production, however, Moore elected to drop this entire subplot.

"I think we all realised the Sagittaron storyline was going to require too much time and effort," Taylor notes, "so we dropped it and took out the references to it in earlier episodes like 'Taking a Break From All Your Worries'. That allowed us to focus on issues we already knew. I definitely think that helped the drama of the piece."

Two of the biggest surprises contained in 'Crossroads, Part I' were also late additions from Moore. The revelation that Laura Roslin had discovered her cancer had returned was a plot twist Moore added to Taylor's script. "I was sitting down doing a rewrite of the finale and I decided, just in that moment, to give Laura her cancer back," Moore explains. "It was an instinctive thing, just like when I wrote Tigh losing his eye in the season première, but it tapped into something I'd wanted to do. When we cured Laura's cancer in the second season, I knew I didn't want that to be a permanent thing. I knew at some point before the end of the series I wanted to bring the cancer back, because I'd always seen it as a key part of Laura's character and who she is.

"The interesting thing about Laura's cancer this time round is that she approaches it very differently," Moore adds. "She doesn't feel the need to hide it like she did in season one. You can see that in the moment where Laura forces Lee to ask her why she's taking

Above: The makers of *Battlestar Galactica* were initially concerned that the trial of Gaius Baltar wouldn't be dramatically strong enough to form the basis of the season finale.

chamalla, which leads to her telling the fleet about her cancer."

Moore also added the break-up of Lee Adama's marriage to Dualla. "I wanted to move things forward and show that Lee was ostracizing himself from everyone around him," Moore says. "I thought it was another way to spice up things, dramatically."

Baltar's trial took place in the series' hangar bay set, which was redressed to serve as a courtroom. Director Michael Rymer found that the courtroom drama offered a welcome change of pace for the series. "I think, for all of us, doing the courtroom stuff was a real highlight," Rymer notes. "It was fun to all be in the same room together, watching the pyrotechnics from the cast."

"Working on the last two episodes of the season was probably one of the most exciting events of my career," Mary McDonnell reveals. "I think Michael Rymer outdid himself. The energy on the set was magical and the whole thing had this feeling that you were being uplifted into a new gear. It was surprising, because you're always tired at the end of the season, but everything became brand new and explosive

SURVEILLANCE: ADDITIONAL

Battlestar Galactica's writing staff had first planned to establish that Laura Roslin was experiencing Cylon visions during the latter part of season two. After this plot thread wasn't pursued, the concept was reworked for 'The Passage' — but the scenes in which Laura learned she was sharing visions with Sharon Agathon did not make the finished cut of the episode.

"We were all set to do it mid-season, but it's a very complicated story to tell so they saved it for the end of the season," Mary McDonnell reveals. "That left the character drifting a bit for a few episodes, because the original plan was that she would then have to deal with the realization she could perceive the world as Cylons do in the latter half of the season."

and interesting. I remember being absolutely thrilled as I sat in the courtroom and watched my fellow actors going at it."

Playing the trial sequences was a similarly memorable experience for the three British actors portraying the defence team. "They called Jamie, James and I the three amigos," Mark Sheppard remembers with a laugh. "We had a lot of fun working together and I think it was funny for everyone to hear us alternate to our usual English accents in-between takes — I mean, I'm playing Irish on the show, Jamie's playing American and James' Baltar voice is actually quite different from his usual accent."

Sheppard reports that his most memorable moments as Romo Lampkin include the scene where he forces Tigh to reveal the shocking circumstances of his wife's death. "It was a hard scene to do," he reveals. "Everyone was so uncomfortable with Romo taking Tigh apart like that. But it's an absolutely tremendous scene and Michael Hogan is just so good in it."

Amusingly, the witnesses to Tigh's testimony include none other than Michael Hogan's real-life wife, Susan. A distinguished Canadian character actress, Susan Hogan plays jury member Captain Franks.

As Baltar's trial continues, the B-plot of 'Crossroads, Part I' reignites the Cylon threat with the discovery that humankind's hunters have been following the fleet for the past two months. It also sets up Part II's revelation of four Cylons being aboard the *Galactica* by establishing that the unknowing Cylons are hearing fragments of the song 'All Along the Watchtower'.

"I had wanted to do something with 'All Along the Watchtower' for a while," Moore says. "When I was working on *Roswell*, I wanted to do an episode all about 'All Along the Watchtower'. It was going to take place in a musical studio and was going to explore whether the aliens in the show had any significance to the song. I wanted the episode to culminate with Bob Dylan turning up and saying that it didn't mean anything, it was just a song. That episode never got made but the idea stayed with me, so I always hoped to use the song on *Galactica*. As early as season one, we talked about the song playing in the background on a jukebox, but we never got round to doing that."

"Ron's idea of using 'All Along the Watchtower' was pretty mindblowing," Taylor continues. "We did debate it in the writers' room. We asked ourselves, 'Is this crazy? Are we jumping the shark?' But personally, I loved it. It feels so weird it has to be right!"

Taylor attempted to build on Moore's use of 'All Along the Watchtower' by suggesting a scene in which the four Cylons were shown imagining themselves at the legendary 1969 Woodstock Festival! "I proposed that in one of my first story documents," he confirms with a grin. "Everyone thought that was a little too crazy!"

'Crossroads, Part I' was initially scripted and shot to conclude with Laura Roslin's announcement that her cancer had returned. But during post-production, several scenes were moved forward from Part II and became the final act of Part I, to guarantee the revelations of the season's final episode had sufficient running time to make maximum impact... ∎

[CROSSROADS, PART II]

WRITER: Mark Verheiden
DIRECTOR: Michael Rymer

GUEST CAST: Mark Sheppard (Romo Lampkin), Chelah Horsdal (Didi Cassidy), Susan Hogan (Captain Franks), Jennifer Halley (Diana Seelix), Keegan Connor Tracy (Young Woman), Leah Cairns (Lieutenant Margaret 'Racetrack' Edmondson), Brad Dryborough (Hoshi), William Samples (Judge #2), Lily Duong-Walton (Hera Agathon), Stephen Holmes (Reporter #2), Alison Matthews (Karen Fallbrook)

"It's true. We're Cylons. And we have been from the start."
— Galen Tyrol, to Saul Tigh, Samuel Anders and Tory Foster

Gaius Baltar feels the trial is going his way following the prosecution's shattering cross-examination of Colonel Tigh and President Roslin, but Romo Lampkin and Lee Adama feel far less confident. After Gaeta perjures himself and tells the court that he saw Baltar willingly signing the death list on New Caprica, Lampkin makes a surprise motion for a mis-trial and calls Lee Adama to the stand.

Lampkin intends to make Lee reveal that Admiral Adama told him that Baltar was guilty and didn't deserve a trial, but instead Lee lists a series of dubious choices made by the *Galactica*'s senior command crew and asks why other collaborators have been pardoned while Baltar stands trial. Lee's passionate comments lead to Baltar being acquitted, on a vote of three to two.

As the *Galactica* nears the Ionian nebula, President Laura finds herself sharing visions of the Kobol Opera House with Sharon Agathon and Caprica Six. Haunted by a strange melody, Tyrol, Tigh, Anders and Tory also find themselves drawn to the same room on the *Galactica*. There, they uncomfortably face the truth — that they are Cylons.

On reaching the Ionion nebula, the *Galactica* and the ships of the fleet all experience a brief power loss which leaves them temporarily unable to make an FTL Jump. When a Cylon armada is detected in the area, the *Galactica* dispatches its Vipers and Lee joins his old crew. While preparing to face the Cylons, Lee pursues an unknown ship and is faced by the return of Kara Thrace. "It's going to be okay," Kara tells a stunned Lee. "I've been to Earth. I know where it is. And I'm going to take us there…"

Jamie Bamber points to 'Crossroads, Part II' as not only a highlight of his time on *Battlestar Galactica*, but also a highlight of his entire career. "The day we shot the scene where Lee takes the stand was the best day I had ever spent in front of a camera to that point," Bamber explains. "It was fantastic for my character and for me personally.

"I felt that scene really nailed the idea that Lee is the conscience of the series — he's defending a man who is hated by the fleet, despite being seen to be betraying everyone.

Above: Samuel Anders is haunted by mysterious music.

Lee holds a mirror of truth to everyone. He sees it's a totalitarian set-up and points out that everyone's guilty in their own way. And shooting the scene was just amazing. At the end I had a standing ovation from the extras, which I'd never had before in my life."

"I thought that was an incredible moment for the character," Ronald D. Moore adds. "I loved the idea of Lee giving a speech about collective guilt and collective shame that highlights the flaws of the system."

Lee's eloquent defence of Baltar follows Gaeta's damning — and false — testimony about the former President's order to execute Resistance members. "That was pretty pivotal to me," Alessandro Juliani notes, "because up to then Gaeta had always done the right thing. He probably thinks he's doing the right thing by lying in the trial, but it shows there are many shades of grey with him. It also shows what a good liar he is."

In early versions of the storyline, the writers planned for Gaeta's false testimony to be discredited before the end of the trial. With the trial apparently going in Baltar's favour at that point, Lee was then set to uncover details of the Sagittaron massacre. Another change from the original storyline concerned Admiral Adama casting the deciding vote in Baltar's favour, which the writers felt validated Lee's decision to defend Baltar.

In early discussions Moore advocated saving the verdict of the trial for season four, but was persuaded by David Eick and the other writers that the storyline needed closure. Another idea was discussed but abandoned, much to the relief of James Callis.

"The trial was originally going to end with Baltar being exonerated, only for him to say, 'I don't give a damn. I'm the son of God!'" Callis reveals. "Baltar was then going to be taken back to prison. I just felt that wasn't going to happen after he had been tortured and imprisoned for so long. It was then changed, so instead we've got some people trying to tell Baltar he's the son of God. I was a lot happier with that."

Baltar's emergence as a "Charles Manson-style cult leader" was first suggested by Michael Taylor. "Ron really liked it," Taylor says. "It was interesting the way it sparked

Above: Laura Roslin, Sharon Agathon and Caprica Six realise that they are experiencing shared visions.

a whole new path for Baltar."

'Crossroads, Part II' also changes the lives of four characters forever as they face the revelation of their true Cylon identities. The nature of that discovery — and the role 'All Along the Watchtower' played in that process — was suggested by Moore. "The idea was that they arrive at a certain point in space where they become aware of who they are and the music manifests that dawning awareness," Moore explains. "The use of the song also taps into the idea of the circle of time — that there is a connection between their world and our world, and certain things repeat themselves."

In an effort to keep the plot twist from being revealed before the episode's transmission, the scene in which the four Cylons are drawn together was not featured in all copies of the script. Dummy scenes that identified the music as a threat to the Battlestar were scripted to disguise the revelation of the Cylons.

"I thought that moment was just great," Rymer says of the scene, which was shot in secrecy. "What was funny was that when those actors first found out their characters were Cylons, hardly anyone was happy about it. Michael Hogan and Aaron Douglas were really put out by it, as was Michael Trucco to a lesser extent — Rehka Sharma was the only one who was pleased about it. But then when they started acting it in that scene, they really got into it."

"The characters' responses to their discovery tells you a lot about their direction in season four," Moore adds. "Tigh says he's a man and tells Adama he's there if he needs him. Tory walks in next to the President. But which of these characters can be trusted?"

Even more secrecy surrounded the mysterious return of Kara Thrace. Not only was her scene absent from scripts, but Katee Sackhoff's name was not even featured on the call sheet.

The exact nature of Kara's reappearance was the subject of intense debate. "The original ending had Lee rushing into his quarters to find Starbuck standing there," Rymer reveals. "Ron wanted two versions of that scene — one where the Cylons were attacking and there was a blackout, and one without that, in case the Cylon attack was too much. Ron had this vague notion

SURVEILLANCE: ADDITIONAL

The version of 'All Along the Watchtower' featured in 'Crossroads' was composed by Bear McCreary. Featuring electric guitar, electric sitar, harmoniums, duduk, yialli tanbur and electric violin, the track is sung by the composer's brother Brendan McCreary (known professionally as Bt4), while the guitarist is Steve Bartek.

"When I first talked to Ron Moore about it, he told me that the idea was that an artist on one of the Colonies somehow recorded a song with the exact same melody and lyrics," McCreary reveals. "Perhaps this unknown performer and Dylan pulled inspiration from a common, ethereal source. So I had to write an arrangement that belonged in the *Galactica* universe rather than our own. Musically, my arrangement is almost entirely an original composition. Only the vocal melody and lyrics remain from Bob Dylan's piece.

"I knew we'd got it right when the finale was at the dubbing stage and David Eick kept asking for the song to be louder and louder in the closing scenes. It reached a point where the engineers just looked at him and said it just couldn't go any louder!

"The feedback to our version of 'All Along the Watchtower' was phenomenal," he adds. "I got as much fan mail about it in the week after that episode aired as I did during the entirety of season three! The way it sounded and was featured in the show really resonated with people."

that she was someone who had changed/transmogrified; the analogy was 'Starchild in *2001*'. I was concerned about that idea, so we talked about another version where Lee Jumps in his Viper and encounters Starbuck in space. That was the ending on my cut, although we shot the other two versions as well."

"Starbuck sitting in Lee's quarters as he rushed to get his flight suit would have been a hell of a jolt, but it would have been difficult to explain that as anything other than magic," says Mark Verheiden. "We definitely wanted to be able to provide a rational, logical explanation for her survival and return, and the Viper reveal was more dramatic."

On learning of the new plans for Kara's return, Gary Hutzel tackled the tricky task of designing a new ship for Starbuck. "I knew Kara couldn't come back in the same ship she was flying in 'Maelstrom', because that ship blew up," Hutzel explains. "So I asked Pierre Drolet, our modeler, to design a Thirteenth Colony ship for us that was familiar in design to the Viper, but was clearly from a different place. It was beautiful. But when I presented it to Ron, he said he wanted to leave things more open, so we went for a brand new, unmarked Viper Mark II that has apparently been manufactured for her."

Hutzel found himself presented with another major challenge during the editing of 'Crossroads, Part II', when Rymer came up with the idea of closing the episode with a shot of Earth. "Michael felt Kara saying 'It's going to be okay' wasn't big enough for the end of the episode and didn't work with the music," Hutzel reveals, "so he and the editor added the traveling-through-the-galaxy sequence from *Contact* to the end of the show. Everyone loved it, but I wanted to do something more unique to *Galactica*, so I came up with the idea of pogo-sticking out of the universe and diving back down. We only had five days to put it together, but I'm pleased with how it worked out."

When asked if Moore had any specific requests about the look of Earth, Hutzel reports that: "The only thing Ron said was that it had to be clearly recognizable as Earth. He wouldn't tell us what year it was supposed to be or anything like that."

"What I loved about that shot was that it holds out a promise to the audience — that we're going to Earth," Moore adds. "It really moves the series forward."

Principal photography on *Battlestar Galactica*'s third season officially wrapped on Thursday December 14 2006. As the finale neared completion, the series' cast and crew became convinced it had succeeded in ending the season on another high note.

"I think 'Crossroads, Part II' is probably the best season finale we've done," Rymer states. "I hadn't had that much fun as a viewer with anything I've been involved with for ages."

"We wanted to do a finale that shocked and surprised and set the table for a different season, and I think 'Crossroads, Part II' achieved those goals," Moore declares. "I thought it turned out really well and put us in a good place for season four." ∎

SURVEILLANCE: ADDITIONAL

If President Roslin's original advisors Billy Keikeya and Priestess Elosha had not been killed off in season two, would either of them have been revealed as Cylons? Ronald D. Moore doesn't have a definite answer. "It's hard to say," Moore muses. "It would have depended on where we took those characters. But I can tell you we never specifically intended to reveal either of them as Cylons. We had only ever talked jokingly about stuff like that."

[THE CHARACTERS]

"Season three brings some fairly profound
events for our characters. These events take them
and their relationships in some very interesting,
unexpected and challenging directions..."
— **Ronald D. Moore**

[WILLIAM ADAMA]

> "I let this crew — this family — disband, and we paid the price in lives. That can't happen again."

After recovering from an almost fatal shooting at the start of season two and reluctantly allowing many of his crew to start new lives on New Caprica at the end of the season, Admiral William Adama begins the third season of *Battlestar Galactica* a changed man. "Adama is a much stronger and much more resilient character in season three," explains his real-life counterpart, Edward James Olmos. "I think he's much more in control of things than he was last season. He's not as quick to allow things to just happen in season three; he takes charge of things in a much more intense way. He's brutally honest with the people around him, and with himself.

"Adama's strength is tested a few times in the season, like the revelation of what happened to one of his pilot friends [in 'Hero']," Olmos continues. "Moments like that completely demoralize him and are just monumental for the character. They're moments of complete torture and pain. But Adama is always able to come out of that and move forward, which is just incredible.

"I liked the changes season three brought for Adama," he notes, "although I have appreciated everything I've got to do in the previous seasons. I do think he's a much more rounded character in season three, but that's primarily because I've played him longer."

Naturally, Admiral Adama's renewed strength and resolve affects his relationships with those around him — especially his interaction with his son, Lee, and President Laura Roslin. In keeping with series head writer/executive producer Ronald D. Moore's belief that "father/son issues never really go away", differences of opinion over such issues as the New Caprica rescue mission and the trial of Gaius Baltar revive Adama's difficulties with Lee. The season also sees Adama becoming closer than ever to Laura Roslin.

"We wanted to play with the Adama/Roslin relationship a little bit in season three," Moore explains. "We wanted to start dancing around the idea that something may be about to happen between them. You can really see that in episodes like 'A Day in the Life', where they're flirting with each other. But we also make the obstacles to them getting together clear and we never intended to take things too far down the road."

"I felt Adama's relationships with the President and Lee grew much stronger in season three," Olmos adds. "But because the stakes become so high, the pendulum swings very quickly from positive to negative in Adama's relationship with Lee. We share moments of joy and also have moments where Adama loses hope in his son. I thought that was extraordinary."

Edward James Olmos' enthusiasm isn't restricted to his character's development in season three. The always straight-talking and forthright actor reports that he's thrilled with the way *Battlestar Galactica* has grown as a series during this season.

"Season three has been a mindblowing experience for me," he states. "I think the season as a whole will be hailed as one of the best seasons of television ever produced. All the episodes have been stellar and when you watch them, you are just caught up in this world that is rivetingly real. I think the intensity of the storytelling has been monumental. The season has been breathtaking and quite unlike anything else on television.

"I feel season three is another jump forward for the series — it's a jump forward from the miniseries and the first two seasons. It's the very best season of television I've been involved with in my life. It's been one of the most remarkable years of work I've ever put in and I'm very grateful to be a part of this. This is something I'll remember forever." ∎

[LAURA ROSLIN]

"Everyone, by law, is entitled to a trial with representation... It is not an option to be discarded at the President's whim."

When Mary McDonnell shot the final scenes of *Battlestar Galactica*'s second season, she knew Laura Roslin didn't have a long-term future as a teacher on New Caprica. "At the end of season two, the producers told me they didn't think it would be very long before Laura was President again," McDonnell explains. "They didn't tell me anything beyond that, so I didn't know how or when she would return to power. All I knew is that I felt Laura would never lose sight of her desire to regain the Presidency — and I was

very happy to find out that the writers agreed with me on that and pursued it in the first episodes of season three.

"It was interesting to explore Laura's involvement with the insurgency and then move her back to being President," McDonnell notes. "As the season continues, we see Laura maturing into a tougher, more complex leader. We also see her struggling with her feelings toward Baltar. Her personal feelings towards him are at odds with how she feels she should operate on a civil level. I think Laura becomes a bit overwhelmed by her anger and frustration with Baltar, and that was wonderful to explore."

Following the exodus from New Caprica, season three also sees the bond between Laura and Admiral Adama growing ever stronger. "Laura's friendship with Adama seems to be sustaining a pretty steady course, despite everything that's happening to them," McDonnell points out. "What I find funny about it is that in the first season, I thought Adama was going to kill Laura!"

Like the latter part of *Battlestar Galactica*'s second season, the majority of season three sees Laura Roslin liberated from the cancer that once threatened her life. McDonnell reports that the temporary suspension of her character's cancer story arc was something of a mixed blessing.

"It certainly made things very different," she says. "For the majority of season three, there wasn't a level of pain and illness underneath everything Laura did, which was fun. I had a lot more freedom of performance and less restraint in my physical energy. You can see that in some scenes, like where Laura unleashes her anger at Baltar."

Season three's two-part finale, 'Crossroads', reveals that Laura's cancer has returned and establishes that she will openly face her predicament as her illness worsens. The finale also sees her experiencing strange visions involving the Cylons. Both these developments thrilled McDonnell.

"I was just blown away by the last two episodes and what they prepared us for," she explains. "They left me extremely excited about what was ahead — more excited, in fact, than I was heading into season three. Those developments opened some fascinating territory for next season and gave me the sense that season four will be extraordinary.

"What I love about the Cylon storyline is that Laura now seems to have a need to communicate with Sharon and Caprica Six, which would open up the world for her a bit. Laura hasn't dealt with the female characters directly very often in the past; she's operated in a man's world with people like Adama, Lee, Baltar and Zarek."

Clearly, the events of season three and its stunning finale have left Mary McDonnell pleased to still be aboard *Battlestar Galactica*. "I feel privileged to be a part of this amazing show," she states. "You know, there are a lot of amazing things on television right now, but we live in such a tough time politically that there's also a lot of whitewashing going on. So I feel really fortunate to be part of a story that's continuing to play directly into the truth of our lives." ∎

[LEE ADAMA]

"The accused has a right to challenge the credibility of witnesses against him. That's just the way it is!"

Jamie Bamber has no doubt that Lee Adama steps out from his father's shadow in the third season of *Battlestar Galactica*. "Lee has to work out who he is as a man, as an officer and as a husband in season three," Bamber explains. "He questions what he has been doing and comes to some pretty stark conclusions. By the end of the season, his worldview has changed and he's perceived differently by those around him. He's no longer 'the Admiral's son'.

"I thought season three was a very dramatic ride that really made good use of the character," Bamber continues. "David Eick once told me Lee is the hardest character to write for on the show because despite his flaws, Lee has to be the moral core, the conscience of the show — and that's not always the most interesting thing to play. So it's a challenge to portray Lee as a moral creature and test his morality. But I think season three does that better than any of the earlier seasons of the show. I was thrilled with what they came up with for the character."

Season three begins with Lee still in command of the Battlestar *Pegasus* — and heavily overweight, thanks to facial and stomach prosthetics donned by Bamber for the first weeks of shooting. While Lee's tour of duty aboard the *Pegasus* ends with 'Exodus', Bamber feels it plays a role in the character's overall development in the season.

"After Lee has commanded the *Pegasus*, there's a sense that he and his father have become equals," he notes. "You can see that in their discussions in episodes like 'Hero' and 'A Day in the Life', where Lee is given more respect by his father.

It's all in the subtext."

Following the destruction of the *Pegasus*, Lee finds himself once again serving alongside Kara Thrace — which paves the way for a reconciliation and affair for the former lovers. Bamber appreciated the opportunity to play the complex drama generated by Lee's forbidden feelings for Kara and how that affected his marriage to Anastasia Dualla.

"From the fleshing out of the miniseries, it was clear in my mind that Kara was the love of Lee's life," Bamber reveals. "I made that decision at the start and the writers took it further. Lee and Kara have always desired each other, but the relationship has never been allowed a go. That's at the bedrock of Lee — he knows that he and Kara feel they are meant for each other but also know either they or their circumstances won't allow it to ever work.

"I don't think that diminishes the relationship he has with Dualla," he continues. "It's a functioning marriage, which Lee feels works. There's something very strong and honest between them. But, tragically, their marriage isn't allowed to work because Lee is living and working so closely to Kara.

"I was surprised by the way Lee and Dualla split up, but I completely understood it," he states. "Dualla is entitled to think, 'Is this the man I married?' And Lee is entitled to think he's committed to doing what he's doing."

While he admits that Lee's weight gain and sudden weight loss early in season "didn't pay off", Jamie Bamber makes it clear he has no such reservations about the rest of the season. He also maintains the dramatic quality of the season's closing four episodes ensured he completed the year feeling that the show was on a creative high.

"When we finished season three, I felt more engaged in the show than I probably ever had been," he declares. "I felt the closing episodes were completely reinvigorating and I love the potential I feel the show has going into season four." ∎

[KARA THRACE]

"Kara Thrace and her special destiny? That sounds more like a bad cover band..."

"**S**eason three is an extremely emotional and eventful season for my character," says Katee Sackhoff, before stopping and giggling at her apparent gift for understatement. After pausing for thought, the ever-bubbly Sackhoff then resumes her review of the season which propelled Kara Thrace on an epic journey that involved love, torture, infidelity, death and resurrection. "At the start of season three, Kara is unraveling and losing her mind. She's trying to hang on to who she is and keep fighting the Cylons after Leoben has spent weeks trying to brainwash her. We then see Kara find unconditional love for this girl she thinks is her child and become willing to give up her own freedom for her. That's a big step for Kara.

"When she returns to the *Galactica*, Kara is emotionally exhausted and drained, and struggles to come back from everything that's happened," Sackhoff continues. "She also has to face Anders and Lee, knowing that she can finally admit she is in love with Lee but isn't good for him, and also knowing she loves Sam. So she's a complete mess all the time. And then she has to face this idea she has a special destiny — which is terrifying for her."

Sackhoff learned that the closing episodes of season three were going to explore Kara's frequently hinted-at destiny during the mid-season production hiatus, when executive producers Ronald D. Moore and David Eick called her to discuss the upcoming episode 'Maelstrom'. "They started the call by telling me they loved me, which I thought was a really bad sign," Sackhoff recalls with a grin. "They then said, 'It's not going to be the end of the character, but we're going to kill you off.' I was shocked! But what was funny about it was that I had heard rumors that one of the main characters was going to die from about the fifth episode, and I had called David and Ron and asked them if it was Kara. They had told me they had no plans to kill me at that point. So it was really interesting the way it went."

Following their surprise revelation about Kara's future, Moore and Eick then made an unusual request about the upcoming storyline. In an effort to preserve the surprise of Kara's planned return, the producers asked Sackhoff not to tell anyone what she knew about Kara's fate and pretend that she believed she was exiting the series.

"They said I couldn't tell anyone — not the cast, not the crew, not even my dad," Sackhoff explains. "That was very difficult, because I had members of the crew coming up to me on the set in tears and threatening to quit! I think everyone was pissed off. So after that, David and Ron started to tell people what was going on."

A few weeks after shooting 'Maelstrom', Sackhoff made an unheralded visit to the *Battlestar Galactica* sets to shoot three top-secret versions of the season finale's closing scene. The scene left the exact nature of Kara's return — and the effects of her resurrection — open for season four to explore.

"I feel Kara's return at the end of the season is amazingly effective," says Michael Rymer, who directed 'Crossroads'. "When she returns, you're left with this 'Whoa!' moment and all the questions are unanswered. There's also a clear suggestion that the character has changed."

The closing moments of season three left viewers keen to find out what exactly those changes entailed — their feelings were shared by Katee Sackhoff. "I think it was probably time for Kara to make a change, so I was excited by the possibilities the finale presented," she states. "To my knowledge, Starbuck as we know her is dead. She's going to be different because of what she's been through. I'm looking forward to finding out what those changes are." ∎

[GAIUS BALTAR]

"I was struggling — struggling to find my place in God's plan... I never intended for some things to happen. Doesn't that matter?"

He began the season presiding over Cylon-occupied New Caprica, facing death threats from human insurgents and the Cylon administrators alike. He ended the season standing trial for genocide, the most hated man in the fleet, after spending months imprisoned aboard both a Cylon Basestar and the *Galactica*. Clearly, then, season three was a trying time in more ways than one for the scientific genius unintentionally behind the destruction of the Twelve Colonies of Kobol, Gaius Baltar.

"The whole season is like a trial for Baltar," says James Callis of his character's exploits in season three. "It's an extremely traumatic season for him. He starts off in the mess he made for himself at the end of season two and things just get worse from there. The season pushes him further than anything that's happened before.

"One of the things we discussed going into season three was the idea that Baltar would be seen to get his just deserts," Callis continues. "We thought that his suffering would create an interesting conflict in the audience, with some people saying, 'The guy deserves it', while others wouldn't be so sure. I thought that was an interesting part of Baltar's journey in season three."

Another intriguing aspect of Baltar's storyline concerns his manipulation of D'Anna Biers (Lucy Lawless), as he tries to uncover the final five Cylons and discover whether he is one of them. While Callis enjoyed playing this story arc, he admits he has never had any real desire to see his character actually revealed as a Cylon.

"From a story point of view, I don't think it would suit our series' mythology to make Baltar a Cylon," he states. "There's no point because this is the man who is partly responsible for the destruction of the Colonies. So I always thought the 'Baltar is a Cylon' storyline was a red herring — although you can never be completely sure what our writers will do!"

Baltar's harrowing emotional journey was reflected in the character's physical transformation as season three progressed. This element of Baltar's development was suggested by Callis.

"I wanted to grow my hair and have a long beard as the season progressed because I thought that was a way of showing the marked change Baltar had gone through," Callis explains. "I thought it was important for him to come back to the *Galactica* looking different, in a way that was indicative of an inner change."

The closing hours of season three complete Gaius Baltar's inner change, with the shamed former President of the Twelve Colonies of Kobol cleared of genocide and being sheltered from would-be attackers by supporters. They also left James Callis intrigued by what the future might hold for his character.

"I think the biggest difference between Baltar at the beginning of season three and the end of season three is that he's no longer running from all the things he's done," Callis notes. "He's no longer in denial, he has a more complex understanding of things — and that makes him stronger. The weakling has been beaten and he's survived everything, and that empowers him.

"What I liked about Baltar's final scene in the season was the way it suggested he was going to become a cult leader. I told Michael Rymer that idea piqued my interest when we were making the finale and I think it will be an exciting direction for the character, so I hope that's where we go in season four." ■

[NUMBER SIX]

"I choose to surround myself with a vision of God's creation..."

The arrival of Gaius Baltar aboard a Cylon Basestar heralds a time of major upheaval for the Cylons — especially the most well-known Number Six model, 'Caprica Six'. "Caprica Six finds her loyalties are really confused and tested in season three," says Tricia Helfer of her Cylon character's development. "At the start of the season, she's feeling some guilt over her role in the destruction of the Twelve Colonies and wants Cylons to peacefully co-exist with humans. She also still loves Baltar, but their relationship is strained.

"After the escape from New Caprica, Caprica Six has a reawakening of her identity as a Cylon and tells Baltar their relationship is over. But then she finds she can't end it and becomes involved in a love triangle with Baltar and D'Anna. Her loyalties then shift again when she helps Sharon escape with Hera. It's a spur of the moment decision, but Caprica Six has always known there's something special about the baby.

"Personally, I found playing Caprica Six kind of confusing this season," Helfer admits. "Things like the love triangle just threw me for a loop. I just did not understand what that came from. I did feel the character kept flip-flopping — but I guess that was the point, because she was so confused herself and doesn't know where she belongs any more. I did think things made a bit more sense by the end of the season, though."

During her time as a prisoner on the *Galactica*, viewers learn that Caprica Six is still experiencing visions of the Gaius Baltar she knew on Caprica. This revelation was made at the request of series head writer/executive producer Ronald D. Moore. "I wanted to keep the idea of 'Head-Baltar' alive with Caprica Six, because I have plans for that storyline for later on in the show," Moore explains. "There was some resistance to the idea internally, but it tapped into where I want the series to go."

In-between playing the original Caprica Six, Helfer continues her role as 'Head-Six' in season three and also appears as various other Six models, most notably the diseased and dying brunette Six that Baltar kills in 'Torn'. Ultimately, Helfer feels these characters didn't really develop Six but instead served the overall Cylon and Baltar story arcs.

"I think season three was an amazing season for the show, but I also think it was the least interesting season for the Six character," Helfer reveals. "I certainly thought there was more for me as an actress in season two. I didn't really have any new characters to play, like the *Pegasus* Six we called Gina, and the end of the season left me thinking that Six is probably the least understood character in the show."

That said, Tricia Helfer is quick to make it clear that she isn't complaining about her work on *Battlestar Galactica*'s third season. And she firmly dismisses the suggestion that she wants to download off the show!

"I love working on *Battlestar Galactica*," she states. "It's an extraordinary show and I enjoy spending time with the people who make it. I was happy to serve the storylines in season three and I think there's a lot of exciting directions the show can go in during season four." ■

[SHARON AGATHON]

"I've made my choice and I know where my loyalties lie."

Throughout *Battlestar Galactica*'s second season, Admiral Adama and the rest of his crew were left pondering the true motives and intentions of the Battlestar's resident turncoat Cylon, Sharon Valerii. From the start of season three, however, series head writer/executive producer Ronald D. Moore decided to take the now-married Sharon Agathon into a different direction.

"When I talked to the writers about where Sharon was going in season three, we all knew we didn't want her to be the woman sitting in her cell any more," Moore explains. "We thought it would be more interesting if we took Sharon to a point where she had built a very close, special bond with Adama, the man she had shot. I really liked the idealism of Adama starting to believe in her. We also wanted to get Sharon back in a Colonial uniform and see what problems that would cause, because it wasn't going to be accepted by everyone."

Sharon's new character arc provided a welcome change of pace for Grace Park, following all the trials and traumas of season two. "Working on season three was very different for me," Park says. "It was lighter and easier in a lot of ways, although there was a part of me that missed the turmoil and drama of season two.

"For me, season three is all about Sharon continuing to build her place aboard the *Galactica*. She's divorced herself from the Cylons and is now searching for peace among humans, but she still feels she has to constantly prove herself and her loyalty. I felt that was a logical progression from season two. I actually thought Sharon's motives were quite clear in season two — the problem was that the humans wouldn't accept that and were always looking for ways in which she would crack."

Season three also removed any lingering doubts about the strength of Sharon's commitment to her human lover, Karl 'Helo' Agathon. "Sharon and Helo totally love each other," Park notes. "In season three, I think you can see their relationship has naturally solidified over time. They absolutely love each other."

Sharon's other primary relationship in season three is the one she shares with Admiral Adama. Park feels that their new bond is much stronger than the Boomer/Adama relationship portrayed in *Battlestar Galactica*'s opening season.

"Sharon's relationship with Adama in season three is much closer and much more intimate than Adama's relationship with Boomer," she explains. "Boomer and Adama had something of a father/daughter relationship, but it was nowhere near as strong as the connection between Sharon Agathon and Adama."

Early in season three, Lieutenant Sharon Agathon gains her own call sign: Athena. "I have mixed feelings about that," Park reveals. "To be honest, Athena felt like a weird name to give to an ex-con! I didn't find that aspect of it totally believable. But at the same time, I was bowled over to get a second call sign from the original show!

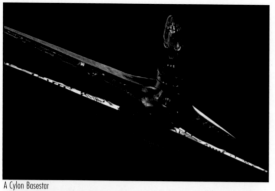
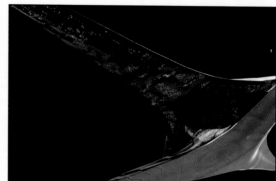

A Cylon Basestar

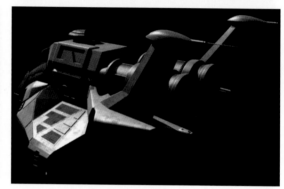

A Raptor

A Viper mk 2

A Viper mk 7

That was funny. It's a nice touch."

In-between playing Athena, Park also continued to portray the Boomer Sharon plus various other versions of Number Eight as part of the Cylon Basestar story arc. "I don't think they write that much for the other Sharons, because when you see them there's a concern the audience might get confused," Park notes. "So we tried to concentrate on Athena and Boomer's storylines in season three.

"I actually felt we gave too much away about the Cylons by stepping inside the Cylon ship this year," she admits. "I felt a lot of mystery was blown by that. But I've also heard some people say they felt the mystery has come back, because that story arc raised more questions than it answered."

Much like her fellow Cylon actress Tricia Helfer, Grace Park readily acknowledges that her role in season three was far less prominent than her work on the series' opening seasons. But she also makes it clear that she remains extremely happy to be a part of *Battlestar Galactica*. "Working on this show is still an amazing experience," she states. "I love the show and the people, and I think the storylines are amazing. So I'm just going to keep making the most of wherever this journey takes me." ■

[SUPPORTING CHARACTERS]

"Any character on our sets has the potential to evolve into something spectacular. Characters like Dualla and Gaeta are prime examples — they were often in scenes as ship's functionaries in the miniseries, but they found attitudes and elements to play that Ron Moore and the rest of us found interesting. We amplified that and found stories for them. Pretty soon the cycle had ramped up to Dualla marrying Lee and Gaeta trying to stab Baltar to death with a pen..."

— Bradley Thompson

At the start of *Battlestar Galactica*'s third season, series head writer/executive producer Ronald D. Moore felt he needed to devise a strong story arc for **Colonel Saul Tigh** and the actor he describes as the "unsung hero of the show", Michael Hogan. By the time the season had wrapped, Hogan felt that Moore comfortably achieved his goal with such plot developments as Tigh's execution of his collaborator wife, Ellen, Tigh's subsequent struggle to come to terms with Ellen's death and readjust to life aboard the *Galactica*, and the shattering season-ending revelation that Tigh is a Cylon.

"Season three is dramatic for Tigh — and dramatic is definitely the word for it," Hogan notes with a wry chuckle. "Ron Moore and David Eick didn't throw me a bone this season, they threw me a steak! It was a very meaty season for me. As an actor, it was a gift to play such challenging material. The season was constantly challenging, both physically and emotionally, but it was also incredibly rewarding. I don't remember dying, but here I am in heaven!"

Hogan found himself challenged from his very first scene in season three, thanks to its revelation that Tigh had lost one of his eyes as a result of Cylon torture. "The first I heard about that was about a month before we started shooting," Hogan recalls. "I phoned David to get an idea of what they were thinking of for Tigh in season three, and he casually told me they were thinking of maiming him in some way. He mentioned he and Ron had discussed Tigh losing an eye. I laughed at the idea and I told David he had to give me some advanced warning if they were going to do that, so I could do some research and prepare for it. I didn't hear anything more about it, until I got the script for the première and saw Tigh had lost an eye! I wasn't chuffed about that.

"From then on, I quickly had to get up to speed on working with an eye patch. It was a tough challenge because as an actor, especially a television actor, your main tools are your eyes and the writers had taken fifty per cent of my tools away from me! But everyone was aware of the problems that raised and I worked closely with Sergio Mimica-Gezzan and then Steve McNutt, our DP, to make sure it would work."

As an actor who believes in the importance of research, Hogan was pleased that he had sufficient notice to research the emotional context of Tigh's arc in season

Above: Saul Tigh has to fight physical and mental scars during Battlestar Galactica's third season — as well as the discovery of his true Cylon nature!

three. "I did a lot of research into Tigh's torture and illness, and how that changes a person," he explains. "I looked at post-traumatic stress syndrome — 'shell shock' as it was called before that, or 'irritable heart' as it was widely called in the American Civil War. I actually thought 'irritable heart' was a great description for what Tigh feels.

"From the beginning, I've always felt Tigh is someone who wanted to have been killed in the holocaust. He would like to disappear in a corner and drink himself to death. But being in command, he has to keep going. He's a career soldier, that's his lot in life and that's what he does. His job is to protect, to allow others to lead ordinary lives. So that's what he has to do in season three — despite the sadness that accompanies the loss of Ellen."

After playing a traumatized Tigh throughout season three, Hogan found himself faced with the biggest surprise of his time on *Battlestar Galactica* when he learned his character would be exposed as a Cylon in the season finale, 'Crossroads, Part II'. "I think I first heard about that from Eddie Olmos and Jamie Bamber," Hogan reveals. "They were messing around on set, humming a song. I asked them what was going on and they told me, 'Haven't you heard? You're a Cylon!' I just said, 'Yeah, right. That's bullshit!'

"When we shot the finale, I actually took the same attitude to it as Tigh does — I took the attitude I didn't know if I was a Cylon or not. I honestly felt very confused when we shot the final scenes, which I think is right because Tigh himself is so confused at the end of the season. I really don't know why the writers decided to make Tigh a Cylon. I think one of the reasons was that it was just so unexpected. But I also suspect the writers thought, 'Give it to Hogan. He'll make it interesting. He won't not do it.'

"In the beginning, I wasn't convinced by the idea — but I also wasn't convinced about Tigh going to New Caprica at the end of season two, which is why they had Adama forcing Tigh to go to the planet. When you look at how that storyline turned out, you can see why I've come to appreciate the writers' wisdom. So when we wrapped season three with the revelation of Tigh apparently being a Cylon my feeling was simply this — whatever the writers want to bring on for season four, bring it on!"

Aaron Douglas makes no secret of the fact he resisted the idea of **Chief Galen Tyrol** being revealed as a Cylon in *Battlestar Galactica*'s third season finale, 'Crossroads, Part II'. "Personally, I took some convincing that Tyrol being revealed as a Cylon was a good idea," Douglas says. "I first got wind of it from Michael Rymer and David Eick, and then I had a really good forty-five-minute phone chat with Ron

Below: Aaron Douglas took some persuading before he saw the exciting possibilities being a Cylon opened up for his character in the next season.

Moore. I told Ron I really liked my character and wanted him to be likeable. I also told him I was concerned turning him into a Cylon would really alienate the series' fans. But Ron made a very strong case and he did make me realize how many exciting possibilities the idea had.

"The interesting thing about making Tyrol a Cylon is that it humanizes the Cylons in a way probably no other character could," Douglas continues. "Tyrol is a true blue-collar guy, a very human person who makes mistakes and has foibles, and so it really blurs the line between humans and Cylons. It will also test how viewers feel towards the Cylons."

Tyrol's discovery of his true Cylon nature another busy season for the Chief. That season begins by establishing that Tyrol has become a leading resistance member on New Caprica and sees him discovering the Temple of Five and resuming his work as union leader, among many other plot developments.

"I got a lot of great stuff to do in season three and that really gave the Chief a lot more depth," Douglas notes. "The season really showed Tyrol's

willingness to do what it takes to protect his people and his family. He puts his life on the line during the insurgency and also in the union episode ['Dirty Hands']. The season also allows Tyrol to show his ability to be a loving father and husband. He gets to show his soft side rather than just go round being grumpy."

Karl 'Helo' Agathon's overriding desire to do the right thing propels the character to the heart of several storylines in *Battlestar Galactica*'s third season. "Season three really builds on the Helo storyline," says Tahmoh Penikett. "Once again, we see this man who is incredibly set in his values, morals and beliefs being willing to do whatever it takes — even be insubordinate — to do what he thinks is right. Episodes like 'A Measure of Salvation' and 'The Woman King' really build on the idea of Helo being a noble person. But the beauty of the show's writing means that he's not perfect. He's a human being who takes chances and makes mistakes and doesn't always know if he's done the right thing."

Season three also establishes that Helo has married his Cylon lover Sharon, in a development that Penikett couldn't be happier with. "Grace and I had both been pushing for that," he reveals. "We left the audience guessing about Sharon's motives in season two, but I always felt that relationship was genuine. I liked the way season three has some tender moments between them, because you can see why they love each other so much; it's this *Romeo and Juliet* story."

Clearly, Penikett is glad to still be playing Helo on *Battlestar Galactica* — especially as the character was originally only set to be seen in the miniseries. "There's not a day I work on this show that I'm not thankful for," he says. "Working on this show has been an incredible journey and I felt season three was excellent for my character."

Anastasia Dualla learns that love doesn't always conquer all in the third season of *Battlestar Galactica*. "Season three is a very trying journey for Dualla," Kandyse McClure notes. "Her love for Lee is really tested and their relationship takes some twists and turns.

"At the beginning of the season, Dualla believes so strongly in Lee: she loves what he represents and recognizes his potential. But Lee's feelings for Kara are heartbreaking for Dualla — especially because Lee's love for Kara is the kind of love Dualla yearns for, so her proximity to it is heartbreaking. That was really interesting for me to explore."

Dualla's relationship with Lee reaches a turning point in 'Crossroads, Part I', which sees her walking out on their marriage. "I was shocked by that at first," McClure reveals. "I had to take some time to wrap my head around it and find what was at the core of that decision. The answer lies with Dualla's principles and her disgust with what Lee is doing during Baltar's trial. She feels she doesn't know who Lee is any more and that there's a chasm between them. So she leaves this man she desperately loves but no longer recognizes."

In the run-up to the season finale, McClure reports that she would have been happy if Dualla had been revealed as a Cylon. "I was hoping I would be a Cylon because all the Cylons are hot!" she explains with a laugh. "But it's interesting for Dualla to be human. She represents the people who still hold on to certain truths and beliefs, and yearn for code and order."

Above: Anastasia Dualla's love for Lee Adama is pushed to breaking point in season three.

Early in the development of *Battlestar Galactica*'s third season, Ronald D. Moore realized that **Felix Gaeta** had the potential for a rich story arc. "I thought Gaeta was a really interesting character in the New Caprica saga," Moore explains. "We had established that Gaeta idolized Baltar and had become his chief of staff and was going to stick by him and work within the system following the Cylons' arrival. But as we really got into season three, we decided that Gaeta would also want to help the insurgency and would start to believe Baltar is evil. I thought it would be interesting to explore the impact and effect of that as the season continued."

Gaeta's revelation as an undercover agent for the insurgency and subsequent struggle for acceptance on the *Galactica* fulfilled Alessandro Juliani's wish-list for season three. "I had asked Ron Moore and David Eick for more juiciness and they definitely threw it my way," Juliani reveals. "The material was very intriguing and I think season three is quite a ride for Felix.

"Gaeta grows up a lot in season three," he notes. "He is not the man he used to be. He grows into a place where he's isolated in the fleet. He has very few friends. He also comes to the conclusion that this idol he worked for and worshipped was nothing more than an empty vessel. I think that haunts him and puts him in a very dark place."

Prior to the broadcast of 'Crossroads, Part II', many viewers speculated that Gaeta would be one of the characters revealed as a Cylon. Was Juliani disappointed when that didn't happen?

"Not really, because I gave up my youthful fantasies of being a Cylon long before that," he replies with a laugh. "Early on, in the miniseries, I wanted Gaeta to be a Cylon because it meant I'd be around for ever. Then in season one there were rumblings Gaeta was a Cylon, because of some of my actions — for instance, a lot of fans online speculated that I'd passed the gun to Boomer when she shot Adama! But I gave up on Gaeta being a Cylon, because I felt it would be too obvious."

Below: The events on New Caprica have serious consequences for Felix Gaeta.

"I thought season three was great for my character, because we got to explore the complexities of juggling between being a mother and wife and having responsibilities on the *Galactica*," says Nicki Clyne of the latest chapter in the life of **Cally Henderson-Tyrol**. "It was great to do so much away from the hangar deck. I enjoyed developing Cally's relationship with Tyrol and seeing the problems they hit when Tyrol tries to take on too much and isn't there for his family. It was also fun to play mom to Nicky. He keeps Aaron and I on our toes because you never know what that baby is going to do!"

Another of Clyne's major discoveries in season three concerned her character's full name. Before season three, the *Galactica* deckhand's full name was unknown and it was unclear if Cally was her first name or surname. "I like being Cally Henderson-Tyrol," Clyne reveals. "I believe the Henderson bit was something the art department and editors came up with, and it stuck; I'd heard it around the set before. There might be discrepancies in the military protocol,

but I definitely prefer Cally being her first name. Her name suits the character and works for me."

At the end of *Battlestar Galactica*'s second season, things did not look good for **Samuel T. Anders**. Not only was the former Pyramid star-turned Caprica Resistance leader desperately ill, but also he had married Starbuck — which led actor Michael Trucco to publicly label his character "a dead man" during the production of the season two finale.

"I was expecting the bullet from the moment I found out about the marriage between Anders and Starbuck," confirms Trucco, a California native and prolific TV guest actor, who was cast as Anders after pursuing the role of Lee Adama in the *Battlestar Galactica* miniseries. "I thought their marriage would dissipate the romantic tension between Starbuck and Apollo, which meant there was only one logical conclusion — Sam Anders dying. So when I was asked to come back for season three and found out that Anders wasn't dying but was actually becoming a more integral part of the story, I was very pleasantly surprised."

Season three proceeded to propel Anders into the heart of the New Caprica Resistance and made him fight to save his marriage to Kara. "I had a great time on season three," says Trucco. "It expanded Anders' role beyond his relationship with

Above: Anders was devastated by his wife Kara Thrace's death.

Starbuck. I loved Anders being a part of the New Caprica insurgency and the tribunals on *Galactica*. I really liked the way it brought up Anders' inner conflict.

"Anders is someone who has been conflicted on every level. Everything this former celebrity athlete thought about his life and his marriage has been turned upside down. He's someone who is forced to become a military man by necessity, rather than through choice. His love for Kara also forces him to constantly try to keep their marriage alive, even when he knows about her affair with Lee. I thought Anders' commitment to Kara was very interesting; at first I thought it was weak and fought it, but then I realized it was complex writing and very true to life.

"Starbuck's death turns Anders' world upside down," he notes. "He is consumed by grief. His overwhelming state is total devastation."

The climax of season three forces Anders to face another shock, in the form of the discovery of his true Cylon nature. "I wish I'd know that Anders was a Cylon much earlier, because I think it would have been useful information to have," Trucco says of this critical plot development. "But I know it works in the context of the series, because Anders himself didn't know he was a Cylon. It's certainly an interesting twist and has left me excited about what it will mean for the next season."

Following his unforgettable début in the second season episode 'The Farm', Rick Worthy was happy to reprise his role as the humanoid Cylon **Simon** during the opening part of *Battlestar Galactica*'s third season. "I feel very proud to be involved with *Battlestar Galactica* because it's such a great show and I do think there's a special status about being a Cylon," explains Worthy, who has also appeared in such shows as *Star Trek: Enterprise*, *Star Trek: Voyager* and *NYPD Blue*. "The Cylons are great characters and I love the way everyone who plays them is so different in their performances.

"Simon is a very distinctive presence among the Cylons," he notes. "He's inquisitive. He's an intellectual. He's someone who will do and say what he thinks he needs to do or say to get what he wants. He doesn't quite get along with everybody in the room — he has a strong idea of how he sees things. I enjoy playing him, although I wish I got to do more with him in season three. I didn't get to explore him in the same way as I did in 'The Farm'. That episode was my favourite experience on *Galactica* to date."

Worthy was initially attracted to the idea of appearing in *Battlestar Galactica* by his love for the original series. "When my agent called me and said there was an audition for a Cylon character on *Battlestar Galactica*, I said, 'I love *Battlestar Galactica*! I used to watch the old show'," Worthy recalls. "I then read the audition material and thought Simon would be a very cool character to play if I could get it right. I hadn't seen the new show at that point, as I didn't have cable TV at the time. But when I did see the miniseries I was blown away — I thought it was one of the best things I had ever seen."

Of the four actors revealed to be playing Cylons at the end of *Battlestar Galactica*'s third season, Rekha Sharma was far and away the most excited. "I was thrilled to find out that **Tory Foster** was a Cylon," Sharma says. "The longer I worked on the show, I found I had a growing desire for her to be a Cylon. On a superficial level, I thought it would be totally fun — I've always wanted to play some kick-ass chick! On a deeper level, I love the way playing a Cylon forces one to go to the heart of the show's mysticism and the commentary it makes on war and our narrow ethnocentric nature and how we objectify our enemies. So when I read an early draft of the season finale I was just so excited! In fact I had to calm myself down, because you never know how much things can change from an early draft and I was afraid the writers might change their minds."

An accomplished stage and screen actor whose TV credits include recurring roles in the Vancouver-based productions *Smallville*, *Dark Angel* and *Da Vinci's City Hall*, Sharma made her début as President Roslin's aide in the late season two episode 'The Captain's Hand'. She was cast as the character after pursuing other roles in the series. "I first auditioned for a couple of smaller recurring roles, one as a captain and another as a 'nugget'," Sharma recalls. "When the role of Tory came up I remember telling my best friend Sarah Lind that I thought the character was strong and smart and had heart, plus a good sense of humour — and I loved that she was working for a female president. By the time the audition came up, I had fallen in love with the character and really wanted the role — I had a feeling working on the show was going to be special. My first day on set confirmed my suspicions were correct."

Sharma points to the episodes 'Collaborators' and 'Crossroads, Part II' as the highlights of her work on season three. The end of the season also left her intrigued by what the future would hold for Tory. "I think that extra Cylon layer Tory now has is going to be very cool to work with," she says. "So the end of season three left me very excited about starting work on season four!" ∎

[PRODUCTION DESIGN]

"Designing on this show is never simple. You always have to design around the architectural style, the cultural history and the nature of the characters involved. You have to think like a Colonial... or a Cylon!"
— Richard Hudolin

The launch of *Battlestar Galactica*'s third season presented the series' production design team with one of the biggest challenges it had faced in the show's run. After successfully defining and developing a startling architectural aesthetic for the Colonial world, Richard Hudolin and his team were required to establish a similarly unique look for a primary Cylon environment: the interior of a Cylon Basestar.

"There was a lot of debate on the look of the Cylon Basestar interiors," says series head writer/executive producer Ronald D. Moore, as he recalls the genesis of the Basestar's interior design. "We knew we didn't want it to look like the *Galactica*. I felt it had to be more 'sci-fi' and not so naturalistic. It had to be alien from the viewers' point of view."

"Designing the Cylon ship was a big deal," production designer Richard Hudolin continues. "It involved a lot of lengthy conversations with Ron Moore and David Eick about what the environment would be and how Cylons communicated. It was interesting because we were basically inventing a whole new society — and then had to make it practical and shoot-able!"

Following a series of discussions in which numerous ideas were considered (including a more overt blending of organic and mechanical elements), Hudolin presented concept artwork of the Cylon Basestar control room and hallways. Featuring a stark and clean quality that contrasted with the visceral look of the *Galactica* sets, the initial concept passes established the core of the Basestar interior's design aesthetic. They also reflected Moore's concept that the Cylons would choose to emulate mankind by

physically interacting with their environment — albeit in a more sophisticated manner than their human creators.

"Ron liked the idea that the Cylons wouldn't just be pushing buttons, pulling levers or looking at screens on the Basestar, but would be controlling the ship in a more interesting way," Hudolin explains. "So we used things like the water, light and projection as the key elements of the Cylon world. Water became a big theme of the design: it's like the lifeblood running through the ship — and you can put your hand into the datastream. That has some religious undertones to it as well, which is another thing that made it interesting."

"We also settled on the idea that the backgrounds would be fairly opaque in terms of the viewer not knowing what the functions or purposes of the lights you're seeing are," Moore adds. "You don't even know where the doorways go or what the rooms are for. That was a way of keeping a bit of the mystery of the Cylon world alive."

The initial concept design drawings of the Basestar introduced the idea of a Cylon Hybrid operating the ship. Hudolin's suggestion was embraced by Moore, who saw The Hybrid as being similar to the 'Pre-Cogs' in the Steven Spielberg movie *Minority Report* and quickly developed The Hybrid into his plans for the Cylon Basestar story arc.

"The initial illustration showed The Cylon Hybrid in the pool," Hudolin recalls. "The idea at that point was that The Hybrid was supposed to look like a failed

Opposite & Above: The interior design of the Cylon Basestar required *Battlestar Galactica's* makers to take the series into a more alien and 'traditionally sci-fi' realm.

Above: The design of New Caprica reflected the look of the original Caprica established by the *Battlestar Galactica* miniseries.

man-and-machine experiment that had been integrated into the ship."

Unfortunately, while everyone on the series embraced the concept of The Hybrid, bringing it to the screen proved more problematic than anyone anticipated. When the first scenes featuring The Hybrid were shot, the series' producers and production designer agreed it wasn't working the way they had originally hoped and revised the finished design. The early Hybrid scenes were then reshot.

"We had a lot of financial restraints on the original version of The Hybrid," Hudolin notes, "and that meant it didn't work the way we wanted it to. But when we redid it, I think it did achieve what we originally wanted."

"The final version of The Hybrid was very similar to an early sketch we did which we abandoned due to the cost," art director Douglas McLean elaborates. "Before we found the final version we had tried other things, like using a fairly dark pool with lit elements. We found a lit pool worked better. We also realized we really needed to show the mechanical and organic mix, and got some specific shots to do that."

As the look of the Cylon Basestar took shape, the production design team was also required to recreate one of the series' most ambitious Colonial environments: the Colonial settlements on New Caprica. The designs for New Caprica took their cue from the earlier work that had been done for season two's closing episode, 'Lay Down Your Burdens, Part II', with the sets being built away from *Battlestar Galactica*'s production base at Vancouver Film Studios, on location at Richmond.

"Recreating New Caprica for the opening four episodes was an enormous start to the season," Hudolin says. "The only thing that made it less difficult was the fact we had designed New Caprica at the end of season two, knowing we would be coming back to it in season three. That meant the design style was in place already. The idea with New Caprica was that they had tried to maintain the design style of the original Caprica, with the limited elements and resources they had at their disposal. I definitely think you can see that on screen."

Another key design project of season three concerned the creation of an important new recurring environment, Joe's Bar. Introduced in 'Taking a Break From All Your Worries', Joe's Bar was conceived to provide a contrast from the series' other primary locations.

Above: Joe's Bar was one of the main new recurring sets built for season three.

"Joe's Bar is meant to be somewhere everyone — pilots, civilians and refugees alike — can relax," McLean explains. "It's a bit more homely than the pilots' rec room, which is fairly small and directly military. It's an informal place that's been thrown together by the people, from materials from the *Galactica*."

"I think Joe's Bar is great," Hudolin continues. "It's been thrown together from odds and ends and has these sleazy, tacky, pinball-type games, like Pyramid X, and a beat-up old Viper hanging above the bar. It's a conglomeration of a lot of different things and the actual set has got a lot of depth and light. That was a really fun one to design."

The closing episodes of season three brought a further critical design project, in the form of the courtroom setting of Gaius Baltar's trial. Constructed in the sound-stage that usually houses the *Galactica*'s hangar bay, the courtroom was initially described as the *Galactica*'s version of New Caprica's Supreme Court.

"That was a real tough piece to design," Hudolin reveals. "In terms of design style I was inspired by Frank Lloyd Wright, whose principals have shaped a lot of *Galactica* since the beginning. I also looked at some courtroom dramas, like *To Kill a Mockingbird*, to see what the great masters had done. But in designing the courtroom, we had to keep the constant limitations of being on the *Galactica* in mind and remember that resources are limited.

"In the end, I thought it worked out really well," he notes. "I think the set has a

Above: The design of the *Galactica's* courtroom was influenced by classic courtroom screen dramas such as *To Kill a Mockingbird*.

great scale and we used some elements of wood in the design, but not too much — just enough to suggest a sense of majesty and an old judicial setting. It was a lot of fun to do and I think [director] Michael Rymer and the actors loved it. It's always good when you give them an environment they like and think is believable."

In-between designing major new environments for multi-episode use, Hudolin and his team also continued to deliver high-impact sets for short-term use. Season three's many memorable temporary sets included the boxing ring created in the hangar bay soundstage for 'Unfinished Business' and the CIC of the Battlestar *Valkyrie* in 'Hero'. The latter set illustrates the series' continued ingenuity, as it was actually a reworked version of the *Pegasus*' CIC.

"In talking to Michael Rymer, we felt we could rebuild and adapt the *Pegasus* set in a way that would suit the *Valkyrie*," Hudolin explains. "So we changed the colour scheme, shot it from one side, avoiding certain angles, gave it a high contrast and took out the doors, and, unless you're looking for it, you don't realize the *Valkyrie* set is actually the *Pegasus* set!"

"Bulldog's stealth ship in that episode is also a redress," McLean adds. "It's a different version of the Blackbird from season two."

As with previous seasons, various real-life locations were redressed to serve as Colonial environments in season three. The homes of William Adama and Socrata Thrace in 'A Day in the Life' and 'Maelstrom' respectively were both actual Vancouver houses, while Kamloops was chosen to double as the algae planet visited in the middle of the season.

"We found quite a few locations this year that we then went into to make our own," Hudolin notes. "We obviously have to do a lot of design work to make sure places fit the *Galactica* universe and also serve the chronology, because both the Adama house and Kara's mother's house were supposed to be in the past on Caprica. Nothing exists that you can just go to and shoot and believe it's *Battlestar Galactica*!

"I thought Kamloops worked really well for us," he continues. "It has a desert, harsh feel and with the colour correction work that Steve McNutt did, I thought it looked fabulous."

Richard Hudolin feels that developments like the series' two-episode trip to Kamloops enabled the production design of *Battlestar Galactica* to continue to impress and grow throughout season three. "I'm very pleased with our work on season three," he states. "I think it's been a great season for us. At worst we've maintained our standards and at best we've improved on them! The season's storylines have been terrific and constantly challenging in what they required from us, and they allowed us to really design for the characters, which is what we do best." ■

Below: William Adama's home in 'A Day in the Life' was a redressed real-life Vancouver house.

[COSTUME DESIGN]

> "The way season three opened up the storylines required a greater variety in costuming than we'd seen before..."
>
> — Glenne Campbell

Above: Glenne Campbell and her team worked hard to costume episodes such as 'The Woman King'; while the nature of Saul Tigh's eye patch was the cause of much debate.

Season three of *Battlestar Galactica* could have been tailor-made to showcase the work of the series' costume department. The season began by unveiling a range of costumes for the occupants of Cylon-occupied New Caprica and continued its fantastic fashion show through such plotlines as the Cylon Basestar story arc and the run-up to Gaius Baltar's trial.

"I lost count of the new costumes we did," costume designer Glenne Campbell notes with a smile. "We added rack space to the ceiling and took over another storage room! It was a really busy season for us — things like the New Caprica storyline, the Cylon story arc and episodes like 'The Woman King' were a lot of work for us. The season definitely brought a lot of fun challenges."

The challenges began with dressing the insurgents and collaborators who feature in the four-episode New Caprica story arc. In keeping with the series' overall commitment to costumes that reflect contemporary and recognizable real-world fashions, the New Caprica Police donned outfits reminiscent of Nazi and fascist uniforms, while the Colonists wore hard-wearing garments that viewers would usually associate with settlers.

"For the New Caprica episodes, we got a huge collection of gently worn clothing from second-hand sources and then broke it down to make it look like the clothes had been lived in to the extreme," Campbell notes. "We kept the '*Gilligan's Island* in space' idea at the heart of the costume design and stayed true to the idea that the characters don't have a lot of clothing — let alone a lot of new clothing — at their disposal.

"I thought the New Caprica Police uniforms looked really nifty, but I honestly don't know where the Cylons got the materials to make them," she admits with a laugh. "The possible answers to the *Trivial Pursuit* question will be: a) the Cylons were spinning and weaving in their spare time; b) Tigh's wife organized a ladies' sewing circle; c) prisoners worked at a reclamation factory where old ponchos were ground up and re-dyed to make into the police uniforms; or d) all of the above!"

Campbell's next ongoing challenge concerned the outfits of the Cylons featured in the Cylon Basestar story arc. "The hardest thing about it for me wasn't clothing the characters," says Campbell, "but actually the logistical challenges of working out what the

Above: Gaius Baltar's prison garb provided a unique challenge for *Battlestar Galactica*'s costume department.

cast and their photo doubles would be wearing in different shots — and getting across to the directors that we don't have an endless stock of clothing to put on people at a moment's notice! But I think it all worked out really well in the end.

"D'Anna and Cavil were both a lot of fun," Campbell notes. "Lucy Lawless had always wanted her character's costumes to stand out and Dean just loved his outfit."

On a far less glamorous note, the closing part of season three required clothing for the imprisoned Gaius Baltar. "Baltar's prison garb was described in the script as thin and ragged," Campbell recalls. "I found the perfect fabric, but we had to make multiple costumes as the fabric was extremely thin and would literally disintegrate before our eyes!"

One of the costume team's more unusual assignments was delivering the eye patch worn by Colonel Saul Tigh during the majority of season three. The eye patch's look was the subject of careful debate between the series' props and costume departments.

"What we wanted to avoid was the 'pirate look'," producer/director Michael Rymer explains. "Michael's performance is so brilliantly on the edge we didn't want to tip it over, so we went with the least theatrical, most normal and 'gritty' version we could."

While Tigh was destined to be revealed as one of the final five Cylons in the season finale, the vision sequences featuring these characters in hooded robes were shot with stand-in actors.

"It was funny, because they were really thrilled to be cast as the final five," Campbell explains with a laugh. "It was a good thing we had fittings before the shoot, as they got all their excitement out of the way and were then able to behave quite somberly on the shooting day!" ■

[VISUAL EFFECTS]

"The visual effects didn't just serve the storytelling in season three — they often expanded it and sometimes even rescued it!" — Gary Hutzel

Above: 'A Day in the Life' was one episode that was greatly enhanced by visual effects.

Gary Hutzel believes that the award-winning visual effects of *Battlestar Galactica* began to enhance the series as never before in its third season. "In previous seasons of the show, the effects had primarily supported the drama," explains Hutzel, who has served as *Battlestar Galactica*'s visual effects supervisor since the beginning of the series. "In season three, I think you saw the visual effects really expanding the storytelling and, on a few occasions, even coming to the rescue of the storytelling by filling in some gaps.

"'Exodus, Part II' is a good example of how we expanded the show: we added things like Hotdog's Viper taking off — I actually gave him his dialogue! — and greatly enhanced both the ground battle and the space battle. The space sequence with Tyrol and Cally in 'A Day in the Life' is another example: that was envisaged as a small sequence of four or five shots and we were able to deliver fourteen shots. That made it bigger and really helped the drama. And the closing shots of the finale ['Crossroads, Part II'] would never have happened if we couldn't have done them in-house; we would have been forced to go with the other ending with Kara and Lee in Lee's room had it not been for our in-house capability. So, overall, we were able to produce more extensive effects sequences in season three, because of the way we built our in-house operation."

Whereas the *Battlestar Galactica* miniseries and first season's visual effects had been produced by external effects companies (primarily the Los Angeles-based Zoic), Hutzel began building an in-house effects department in season two. He used season three to build the series' in-house effects capability much further and opened a new *BSG* VFX office in Los Angeles, to complement the in-house effects work produced by the team based above Stage D at Vancouver Film Studios.

"We produced about sixty to seventy per cent of season three's effects in-house,"

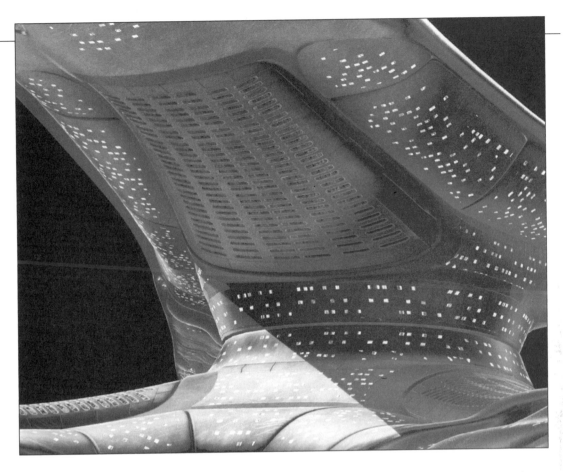

Above: The exterior appearance of the Cylon Basestar was redesigned for season three.

Hutzel reveals. "I believe we produced all but two or three of the effects shots for the closing ten episodes of the season; the remainder of the work was done by Atmosphere VFX. Atmosphere was a very understanding partner and we've continued to have a great relationship with them.

"By building our in-house operation, we found we were able to produce more extensive sequences and were less constrained in financial terms than we were in earlier seasons. I think that really benefited the show. It also helped us to know that Atmosphere were there if we needed them."

Hutzel reports that the development of an in-house effects department was not meant to have any impact on the core 'hand-held camera, documentary' style of *Battlestar Galactica*'s visual effects. The series' computer-generated imagery (CGI) also continued to be primarily produced with the software packages Lightwave, Digital Fusion and Combustion. One major development that did take place, however, concerned the digital models of the Cylon Basestar and the series' other primary vessels.

"We redesigned the look of the Basestar for close-up shots, because of the style we were taking with that storyline," Hutzel explains. "When Ron Moore came up with the idea of turning the scenes aboard the Basestar into lyrical, slightly surreal sequences with cross-dissolves and everything else, I felt we should continue that in the exterior shots and make them long, slow moving and lyrical. Ron agreed, but then it became necessary to redesign the Basestar to give it additional surface detail for the close-up shots.

"In doing that, we developed the Basestar's functional organic structure. We also tried to make the surface of the Basestar more flesh-like; for the explosion in 'Exodus, Part II', we went for a ripping-of-the-skin effect, rather than an explosion. By the end of the season, the surface had moved towards a more dolphin-like skin. It's very subtle, but the modification is there.

"We also upgraded the other models in-house to take advantage of the Lightwave 9.2 upgrade and its enhanced rendering capabilities," Hutzel continues. "That allowed us to do more sophisticated lighting and also add some exterior lights to the *Galactica*, which gives it a little more scale."

Battlestar Galactica stayed at the cutting edge for the late-season three instalment 'Maelstrom'. This episode sees the series generating visuals with an upgraded version of Vue, a 3D terrain effects package more usually associated with films such as *Pirates of the Caribbean: Dead Man's Chest*. "The version of Vue that had just come out featured cloudscapes, so we started to play with that for 'Maelstrom'," Hutzel explains. "It was extremely challenging to get Vue to generate the cloudscapes we

Below: A Cylon Raider takes flight.

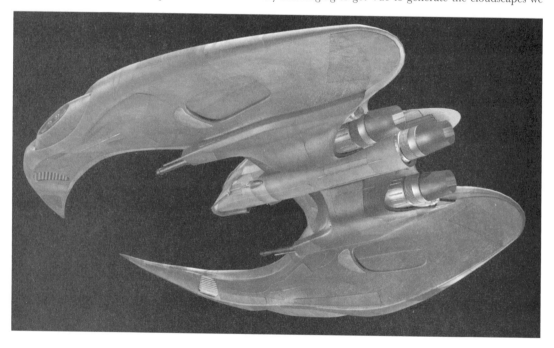

wanted for the episode and deliver it on time, but I thought the results were worth it. It was good for us and very good for the series."

Hutzel points to 'Maelstrom' as one of the most memorable episodes of season three from a visual effects perspective. He also selects the Cylon Centurion sequences in 'Rapture' as another highlight. "There's some complex work in those scenes," he notes. "I think we did about ninety per cent of the Centurion stuff in-house. They could have just been, 'You see the Centurions... they get blown up!' Instead, we put in as much complexity as we could; for instance, we did some complicated animation with them loading up their rockets.

"Those shots allowed us to develop more personality for the Centurions, which is interesting because Ron Moore wasn't originally interested in that," Hutzel adds. "We made them expressive and interactive and capable of independent thought. So that's another way we've tried to enhance the storyline."

Another of the effects department's services to the Cylon Empire concerned the visualization of multiple models of humanoid Cylons. "We did some of that with visual effects, but actually did a surprising amount of it with body doubles," Hutzel reveals. "Some directors, like Michael Rymer, prefer to use doubles. There's a scene between Boomer and Athena that uses doubles and is done so seamlessly that it plays beautifully. So we don't always need to use effects for that stuff."

Clearly, Gary Hutzel feels that everyone can see that *Battlestar Galactica*'s visual effects shine brighter than ever in the series' third season. "I'm very proud of all the work my team has done on the series in season three," he states. "There are a lot of shots that — given the time and money constraints — were simply unreasonable to do, but the people I have working for me made it happen anyway! That was fantastic.

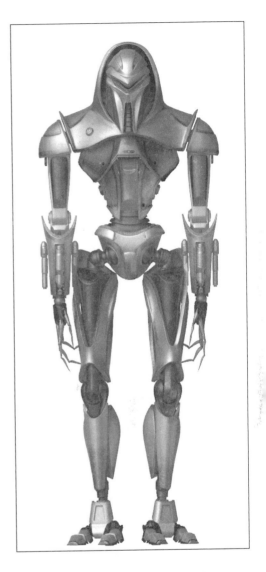

Above: The visual effects department worked hard to give more personality to the Cylon Centurions.

"We worked harder than ever to get the effects right this season. I never wanted the show to get complacent — and neither did David Eick or Ron Moore. They are pretty picky about the effects. They don't just let anything go on the air; they want the effects to be really integrated into the storytelling and the show. But I think we've ensured that and it's resulted in season three being better than anything we've done before, both from an effects perspective and an overall show perspective." ■

[MUSIC]

"The producers didn't want the music to sound the same as the previous season. They wanted it to continue to evolve, which was a wonderful opportunity for me..." — Bear McCreary

Above: Bear McCreary.

From the evocative song that accompanies the season première's opening moments to the uniquely mesmerizing reworking of 'All Along the Watchtower' that drives the season finale, Bear McCreary's musical exploration of the *Battlestar Galactica* universe grew and developed in exciting and imaginative ways during season three. "I thought there was an incredible evolution in the music between season one and season two, and I feel that evolution continued even further in season three," says McCreary, who composes, orchestrates and conducts the series' score. "I think the music is more mature and complex in season three. It's also put together in more interesting ways and just sounds better, because of the opportunities I was given to explore and expand things.

"On a lot of TV shows, a composer is asked to find the sound of the show as quickly as possible and is then asked to not deviate from it. On *Battlestar*, Ron Moore and David Eick encourage me to introduce new elements and totally different styles of music. That's been wonderful. I've also been shocked by some of the new ideas they themselves have brought to the table — like doing a *Galactica* version of 'All Along the Watchtower' and using piano music on the Cylon Basestar. My initial reaction to those ideas was, 'Is that going to work?' But I think they turned out beautifully."

Season three allowed McCreary to expand on earlier pieces of incidental themes as well as introduce completely new tunes, styles, instruments and ideas into the *Battlestar Galactica* audio mix. While McCreary points to 'Exodus', 'Unfinished Business', 'Dirty Hands' 'Maelstrom' and the season-ending 'Crossroads' as the episodes he found most memorable to score, he insists that every instalment was a pleasure to work on.

"Season three was the most rewarding season for me yet," McCreary states. "It was the most challenging too. There were a lot of sequences that were really difficult to get through — like Colonel Tigh's execution of his wife and the scene where everyone returns to the *Galactica* after the escape from New Caprica. Scenes like that were so big and powerful and moving, there was so much pressure on me to come up with a piece of music worthy of them. It was hard to write the music for those scenes. But when you get through it, you come up with music that's better than the typical TV music score."

At the start of season three, McCreary began blogging about his *Battlestar Galactica* experiences on his website, www.bearmccreary.com. "It's funny, when I started the blog I didn't know if anyone else would be interested," he reveals. "I started it because every *Battlestar Galactica* episode is a little adventure of its own, and I wanted to document my experiences for myself. I thought when the series is over, I would then be able to look back and see the things that went into constructing these scores, because they're very well thought out, especially for television.

"But since I've been doing it, I've had a lot of feedback from *Battlestar* fans, which has been great. What I like about doing the blog is that I can go into a level of detail that just wouldn't belong anywhere else."

Above: A sample of McCreary's musical composition for the series.

In addition to spawning a highly informative blog, McCreary's work on *Battlestar Galactica* has also inspired a series of popular soundtrack albums. "I'm very proud of the albums," he says. "They're a great opportunity to take some twenty hours of music and condense them to the best hour. When you do that, I think you get an album that really plays well.

"I've been thrilled that the albums have been received so well," he adds. "I feel lucky to have had the opportunity to release them."

After three seasons of scoring *Battlestar Galactica*, Bear McCreary's enthusiasm for Colonial composition remains as strong as it's ever been. "*Battlestar Galactica* is such a cool show to work on," he states. "Every aspect of the show — the writing, effects, editing and performance value — is top notch and I'm glad the music really seems to fit in there." ∎

[INTO SEASON FOUR]

"There's going to be a strong sense that the series is moving into its climactic chapters in season four..." — Ronald D. Moore

With its third season, *Battlestar Galactica* consolidated its position as one of the best series on television. Critics in publications ranging from *Entertainment Weekly* and *TV Guide* to *National Review* and *Time* continued to rave over the gritty sci-fi drama. The Peabody Award-winning series also collected numerous new accolades, including being named as one of the Ten Outstanding Television Programs of the Year by the American Film Institute (AFI) for the second year running.

By the time the season reached its astonishing climax, critics and viewers alike had no doubt that *Battlestar Galactica*'s third season had been a worthy continuation of the series. Their belief in the series' creative success was shared by *Battlestar Galactica*'s leading lights, executive producers Ronald D. Moore and David Eick.

"Overall, I thought season three was very strong," Moore says. "I was extremely happy with the beginning of the season — the whole New Caprica storyline and how that played out — and I loved the way it launched us into things. I thought we got a lot of great moments out of that storyline.

"I did feel we hit some soft spots in the middle of the season," he admits. "We did some stand-alones, which have always been problematic for us. But once we got to 'Maelstrom', I think everything ramped up and I thought the trial turned out really well. So I was very happy with the season. It was the riskiest season we had done to that point. We took a lot of gambles and really pushed the show in new directions."

"I feel we hit higher highs in season three than we had hit in previous seasons," Eick adds. "I also really feel season three, in epic terms, was the boldest season we have done so far."

Sadly, the incredible high quality of *Battlestar Galactica*'s third season was not initially reflected in its US viewing figures. After premièring with a 1.8 Nielsen viewer rating, which was lower than season two's 2.0 average episode rating, season three's ratings proceeded to decline — prompting a mid-season move from airing on Friday nights to Sunday nights. While the new timeslot led to an eight per cent increase in viewership, the series continued to be widely perceived to be struggling in the ratings.

"We did hit some specific challenges in season three," says Eick of the series' performance in the ratings. "By moving the start of our season to October, we were up against broadcast network television fall premières and baseball premières, so we had much tougher competition. We also hit the problem of being on a network and targeting a demographic that research shows is generating more and more of its viewership by alternate means — like DVDs, iTunes and TiVo. Those things made it harder to be specific in terms of traditional viewing figures."

Fortunately, after lengthy discussion and negotiation, the US Sci Fi Channel officially announced it had commissioned a fourth season of *Battlestar Galactica* on February 13 2007. Although Sci Fi's initial announcement cryptically stated that it had committed to "a minimum of thirteen hours", the network confirmed shortly after that the order had increased to twenty episodes plus a TV movie.

Despite the lateness of Sci Fi's renewal order, Moore and Eick had remained confident that *Battlestar Galactica* would live on into a fourth season and had always based the end of season three around that assumption. They also began developing ideas for season four long before the series' official pick-up, to ensure everything would be on track for the start of production in May 2007.

"Season four is going to be much more about the search for Earth," Moore says of what lies ahead for the series. "As you'd expect from the end of season three, it's also about the mystery of Kara Thrace — who is Kara and what can they believe about her? We have four Cylons with a secret on the ship. How are they going to deal with that? Do they have an agenda? Will they start worrying about whether they're going to go off and hurt someone? How do they keep an eye on one another? Who can they trust? Those are some of the key questions at the start of the season.

"We're going to go back into the Cylon world a bit in season four," he continues.

Above: *Battlestar Galactica's* fourth season promises some "extremely unexpected twists and turns" for the *Galactica's* crew, according to Michael Angeli.

"We go aboard some of the Basestars again. There's going to be a political change that starts happening in the Cylon world. There are different alliances formed and broken among the Cylons and also the humans. Laura's cancer has returned too, so we're going to play her treatment in a much more real and upfront way than in the opening seasons."

"Season four is going to do things you would never expect us to ever do," co-executive producer Michael Angeli adds. "There are some extremely unexpected twists and turns. We're going to lose some characters and we have some political manoeuvring that I think will surprise everyone."

To compensate for delaying season four's première until early 2008, Sci Fi announced that its two-hour *Battlestar Galactica* TV movie would air in the fall of 2007 — with a DVD release to take place around the same time. "Universal [Sci Fi's parent company] originally came to us with the idea of doing a movie," Moore recalls. "We felt we didn't want to pick up the cliffhanger in the movie and then leave people waiting again for the new season, so we knew we wanted to do a stand-alone. From there, we quickly started talking about doing the *Pegasus* back-story, in a way that involves our characters and also sets up events in season four."

While Moore and Eick succeeded in getting an order for both season four and a *Battlestar Galactica* TV movie, the proposed prequel series *Caprica* remained in development and uncommissioned by Sci Fi. When asked why *Caprica* wasn't immediately picked up on the back of *Battlestar Galactica*'s success, Moore plays down suggestions that the radical 'sci-fi soap' spin-off he developed with Eick and writer Remi Aubuchon was too dark or too challenging for the network.

"I think the main problem was that the network was afraid of the serialized nature of what we were trying to do," he says. "The serialized nature of *Galactica* has definitely hurt the ratings of our repeats, as happens with all serialized shows. *Caprica* was designed specifically to have a very serialized storyline and I think they baulked at that and decided they didn't want to go down that road at that point.

"There's still a possibility it will get made one day," Moore adds. "There continues to be talk of a TV movie/backdoor pilot."

Whatever the future holds for *Caprica*, Ronald D. Moore insists that he doesn't intend to allow anything to stop him and his colleagues from enjoying working on *Battlestar Galactica* as it enters its fourth season. "I do feel I'm moving into a bittersweet stage on the show, as I know it will end in the not too distant future," he says. "Dramatically, we know we're moving towards the end of the show and the knowledge this journey will soon be over fills me with a sense of loss, even though there's a great feeling of accomplishment.

"When we've written the final chapter of *Battlestar Galactica*, we're all going to be able to look back with pride at this thing we've recreated and remember how it touched a chord with people out there," he states. "That's going to be very gratifying. But right now I'm just trying to enjoy it for as long as it lasts." ■

ALSO AVAILABLE FROM TITAN BOOKS

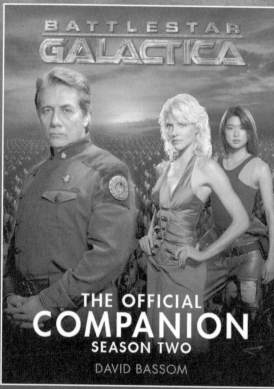